To Robert,
Merry Christmas!!!..
God Bless!

Jer. 29:11

Taming

Tigers

By Dan Stockdale

ISBN-10: 0-9794123-0-7
ISBN-13: 978-0-9794123-0-1

Printed in the United States of America

TABLE of CONTENTS

DEDICATION

This book is dedicated to my wife, Stacey, and son, Daniel. They patiently tolerate my allure with exotics. They overlook monkey bites from baby primates, they worry about Dad when I am working with large cats, they listen to my stories about grizzly bears, and through it all, they have not insisted that I go to therapy (yet!). I love you both dearly, and I would not be able to do what I do without your love and support. Thank you for being the best wife and son in the world!

Also, thank you to my parents, Wayne Stockdale and the late Reba Stockdale, who bought their young, adventurous, insistent son a tiger pillow at an Exxon station, I believe it was along the Pennsylvania Turnpike in the late 1960s or early 1970s, on a family trip to the cabin on Uncle Dave's farm. It is my first memory of tigers and is probably the reason I developed such a passion for them. You two are the greatest parents a boy could ever have.

My Son & Wife - Daniel & Stacey Stockdale

ACKNOWLEDGEMENTS

I have to begin by thanking Mark Oliver Gebel, son of the late, great Gunther Gebel Williams of Ringling Brothers, for getting me started on this tiger journey. Mark and Gunther are two of the most famous exotic animal trainers in history, and it is my privilege to have interviewed Mark. This book has been in the making since 2003, and Mark was there in the beginning with great ideas that are threaded throughout. Thank you Mark for your insight and interest!

I also want to thank Jeff Harrod for his willingness to help, for his readiness to drive for hours on end to our first official "Taming Tigers" event, and for the knowledge that he has so willingly shared. He is even succeeded in getting me past my anxiety with snakes. Okay, not really! But at least I can tolerate having a six foot boa around my neck now. Jeff operates a facility in Palmdale, Florida called Vanishing Species. If you ever have the opportunity, give him a call and arrange for a personal, guided tour. Jeff also holds the record for the largest alligator ever captured in Florida and the largest python ever captured in Florida. He is a true wild man!

I also want to thank Jarrod Davis from Tails of the Wild. Jarrod patiently worked with my photographer and me to capture tiger, primate, and macaw shots that took some effort. At the time, Jarrod was living in Tennessee with eight of his striped friends and a bevy of other critters. Nowadays, Jarrod calls Florida home. He was there and good-naturedly accommodated my first hands-on encounter with a tiger. His background includes stints with many of the most well-known acts in America! Thanks, Jarrod!

I also want to thank Brian, Vikki, Eric, Chris, Greg, Jet, Tina, and Eddie. Chris and Greg, you guys have been particularly helpful. Thanks for the time you have spent chatting with me, and especially the evening in Chicago on the loading dock overlooking Lake Michigan. That evening in September 2006 helped me solidify my approach to this book. Thank you. All of the gang in California was great to work with, and you each truly set the standard for safety and animal welfare in a business that is very demanding.

Also, thanks to Sara, Chris (by the way Chris, we have got to finish our business plan for clicker training!), Chelsea (with an "a"), Chelsey (with a "y"), Michelle (go "Team Tiger!"), Tracy, Mars, Mona, and Wendy. Our three weeks together in the high desert with temperatures of 105+ were grueling, but you guys were a great team to work with. By the way, Michelle, "Who cut this meat!?" Good luck in all you do! If any of you are reading this, then you remember lunch in Agua Dulce. Thanks for paying me back by buying the book.

Last but not least, thank you to *you*, the reader, for wanting to make a difference in your life and for believing that there may be a morsel of knowledge in these pages that may help you as you forage life's jungle. The *Taming Tigers* approach is not always the quickest or easiest, but I have found it to be the best and most productive. I hope you find this book to be a great read and resource.

Finally, and most importantly, I hope you finish this book with a newfound respect for all of our endangered species, but specifically our tigers. Their future rests in our collective hands. Their numbers in the wild are dwindling quickly. The need is urgent. We need your help. Please do your part to ensure their survival.

A NOTE FROM THE AUTHOR

I love exotic animals and learning how the relationships between humans and animals can create dramatic results! To provide you with some background, I have a bachelors degree in psychology, am completing a masters in corporate communication, have graduated from a professional Exotic Trainer & Husbandry course, have studied behavior extensively, and have a significant amount of 'hands-on' time with various species. I work with tigers daily. Most of the time they are in organizations, sometimes they are the four-legged type in arenas. My life is exuberant and I have been truly blessed to have many periods of experience with numerous organizations as well as various species, including tigers, over the past two decades.

My experience with all animals has given me keen insight into their minds and instinctive behavior. I have also had the opportunity to know, interview, and train with some of the finest exotic animal trainers in the world, namely, the folks listed in the Acknowledgements. They have each contributed bits and pieces that, when combined with my own knowledge and business background, comprise the *Taming Tigers* approach to personal and business relationships.

In regard to the "textbook" definitions of psychology terms used in these pages, know that my intent is to communicate concepts as they can best enable you to apply them to your daily lives. Thus, I use terms at times in a manner that would likely frustrate an academician. Please understand that my intent is to write a useful book in layman's terms, not a textbook.

In regard to the names and examples I have used in this book, I have changed the names and circumstances enough so that no one could easily identify them. I have not, however, changed the essence of the stories and the lessons to be derived.

I can't conclude my Notes without tipping my hat to the individuals who work day-in and day-out in the animal industry. *Many* of them are members of the American Association of Zoo Keepers. *All* of them make tremendous personal sacrifices to care for the animals entrusted to them. Many times they work for low pay, sacrifice holidays (yes, including Thanksgiving, Christmas and New Years Day), and toil in steamy hot or frigid cold conditions just for the sake of the animals. Animal people are amazing! Our world is a better place because of you. Thanks for all you do!

As I am sure you are aware, many schools and businesses have adopted the fearless tiger as their mascot. Let me challenge every organization represented by the tiger to annually contribute funds to a worthy organization involved in the preservation of the animal that so greatly defines the spirit of your group. If every school and business with a connection to the tiger would do so, we could, as a community, save a species.

Although it may seem obvious, I must add a quick note regarding ownership of tigers as pets. I fully understand the attraction of a tiger. They are spectacular animals. But large cats should only be kept by organizations and individuals with the appropriate experience and resources to provide a lifetime of care. Cute as they may be as cubs, they are not "pets" and should not be kept as such. Enjoy them in safe, professionally managed environments.

Finally, I have used the words "taming" and "training" interchangeably throughout this text. Taming means to "domesticate or make docile," whereas training means "to teach or learn." Please understand that, in the real world, real tigers *can't* be tamed. Trained? Yes. Tamed? No. They are wild creatures at heart and they always will be, regardless of what we may naively think as humans.

That being said, however, the text seems to flow better by using the words interchangeably. Please indulge me by accepting my liberal use of literary license in this regard.

Taming Tigers

Tigers

By Dan Stockdale

Preface:

Conserving Our Tigers, Our Organizations, and Our Relationships

You will find facts throughout this book about the magnificent wild tiger. You may not realize that several species of tiger are already extinct, and every species remaining is critically endangered.

Fifty years ago, eight subspecies of tigers, numbering 100,000 strong, roamed the world. Now only five subspecies remain, as the tigers living around the Caspian Sea became extinct in the 1950s, and Balinese and Javan tigers disappeared by 1972. Today, only 20 to 30 South China tigers, at best, remain in the wild, although recent reports indicate that these, too, may well be extinct.
Only 5000 tigers are thought to survive in the wild in the entire world. In fact, today more tigers live in captivity than live in the wilderness. Unfortunately, the wild tiger could vanish from the earth forever in as few as five years.

Tigers, however, are at the top of the food chain and should be flourishing. As a matter of fact, man is a tiger's only predator! But, consider the factors that have led to its demise: human population increases and resource overuse have led to the loss of natural tiger habitat, and the use of tiger parts in traditional Eastern medicine continues to be a threat.

Habitat loss and degradation due to agriculture and logging seriously threaten tiger populations. Just one example is a multi-million dollar tiger reserve built in the 1970s near New Delhi, India. The park was considered a triumph for preservation and was an instant tourist sensation.

1

Dan Stockdale

As human population in the area increased, however, pressure on natural resources also increased, and the private land owners surrounding the reserve began to cut wood and graze their cattle there. Gunfights between rangers and cattle owners ensued as thousands of head of livestock took over the protected tiger habitat. Poachers killed so many tigers that today visitors to the reserve rarely see the cats.

In addition to habitat loss, man's uncontrolled hunting has decimated tigers' food sources, such as deer and wild pigs, two primary prey for tigers.

Even more difficult to manage is the use of every single part of the tiger in traditional Asian medicine, a practice that dates back a millennia or more. Although no scientific evidence shows that these remedies work, a burgeoning population and a worldwide resurgence in interest in Eastern medicine has made harvesting tigers even more rampant.

Tiger parts also serve as trophies and trinkets to ward off evil spirits. As illegal trade in tiger parts is forced underground, illicit tiger farms, where tigers are raised and "harvested," are said to have sprung up throughout Asia. Although it is illegal, officials estimate that tigers in India alone are being killed at the rate of one per day.

Incentives for poachers have also greatly increased. Because a poacher can charge up to $115 a pound for tiger bones - as much as some villagers earn in a year – poaching can be difficult for the poor to resist.

The main markets for illegal animal derivatives are China, Taiwan, Korea, and Japan. But tiger powders and potions can be bought throughout the USA, Europe, and the UK, and at least 120 outlets sell tiger derivatives in Australia alone.

For more information on tigers, their endangered status, and what you can do to help, visit the following websites and consider making a

2

donation of money, time, or talent to help save these incredible creatures.

World Wildlife Fund:
http://www.worldwildlife.org/tigers/

National Wildlife Federation: http://www.nwf.org/wildlife/tiger/

Smithsonian National Zoological Park
http://nationalzoo.si.edu/Animals/GreatCats/BreedingTigers.cfm

Save the Tiger Fund
http://www.savethetigerfund.org/

You may be thinking, "That is important to know, and I would really like to help, but what does conservation of tigers have to do with me?" Just as you may have been unaware of the plight of the wild tiger, you may have never before considered the necessity for conservation in your own world.

In many communities – maybe even in yours – when people develop an obsession with progress – economic development, increasing tax revenues, and building infrastructure – they tend to forget about the animals that are displaced, ignore the deterioration of natural habitat, and completely disregard long-term environmental consequences. A shopping mall or new subdivision may seem important now, but it can lead to extinctions of wildlife and serious effects on the quality of life for generations to come.

We are well past the point where we can continue to consume resources and exploit our environment, turning a blind eye to the future.

Conservation is just as important in your business life and household as it is in your community and in the world as a whole. If you are not doing the right things in your corner of the world at home or work – your "tribe," if you will – you are simply not going to thrive. You can even threaten your own survival, as a business or family, by neglecting to center your attention where it must be focused. But you need not let issues – even the big ones – get to the point where you face extinction!

Deliberate conservation in all areas of your life will not only ensure your continued existence, it will allow your life to flourish. You see, you can't let nature take its course and blindly believe that all will be well. It will not! You must be proactive in orchestrating your future – personally and professionally.

You don't want to merely survive; you must thrive in all you do! Don't put conservation off because you are too busy and tired; we need to be inspired!

Taming Tigers will inspire you and teach you how to conserve and preserve, to be proactive, not reactive. It will help you to take control, not be controlled. It will offer you techniques that have been used for centuries to train tigers and show you how they can help you to achieve personal and business success in life!

That is a pretty weighty promise, isn't it? But I assure you that if you follow the principles you are about to learn, it will indeed change your approach to your personal and business relationships!

We may not be able to save all of the tigers in the wild, but I know we can tame your beasts. Now, let's tame those tigers!

TIGER TALKING POINTS

1. What are the main reasons for the decreases in tiger population?

2. How many species of tigers originally existed?

3. How many remain today?

4. Which one of the remaining subspecies is currently the most endangered?

5. What does conservation of the environment have in common with conservation of your home and business?

Dan Stockdale

SECTION 1:

Discover the Tiger Tamer Within!

Dan Stockdale

Let's just learn to get along!

Chapter 1: Taming Tigers

A Technique in Human Relations

*"Know what you value, be willing to take a risk, and lead from the
heart – lead from what you believe in."*
-Alan Keith, Former VP of Business Operations, Hanna-Barbera

If you ran across a wild tiger or two in the course of your daily life,
you would soon learn the basic rules of tiger taming...or else!

In fact, you *do* encounter tigers every day – in the form of difficult,
upset people and potentially danger-fraught personal and professional
situations. Wouldn't a few ideas from a professional tiger tamer, a
person who really knows his tigers, help?

Imagine you've been given the opportunity to hang out for a day or
two with me while I work with a 500 pound Bengal tiger named Taj.

First, observe the tiger tamer's *calm, matter-of-fact approach.* He
does not intend to let a few wild growls upset him and interfere with
the job at hand. He knows that tigers hiss and growl on occasion,
especially when they are feeding and someone approaches, and the
tiger tamer accepts that response as part of a tiger's natural behavior.
He does not try to change their natural instincts, nor does he let their

behavior affect him. He has a goal to accomplish and he will do just that.

Notice, too, his air of *quiet confidence*. You can tell he has dealt with tigers before. The tigers can tell, too. No matter how big the tigers are or how fiercely they growl, you get the feeling that the tiger tamer has the situation well in hand. He has a healthy respect for the beasts combined with an attitude of love and compassion.

You will also recognize the *mutual trust* that the tiger tamer has intentionally built into the relationship since his first encounter with the animal. Sure, the tiger could hurt him, but there is no reason to, because the tiger knows the trainer has its best interests at heart.

The trainer knows his tigers well and has worked to develop the relationship. His tigers share the mutual affection. Not to worry, the tamer also knows they are *tigers* – wild animals - and is always vigilant, but he also takes pleasure in the trusting relationship he has shaped.

The tamer does not take the tiger's wildest growls personally. If it is snarling at the trainer, it is because the trainer's a trainer! It would do the same to anyone else in that job.

No matter how fiercely the tiger snarls or growls, the tiger tamer does not ever growl back. He never shows any emotion except pleasant confidence. *His business is to tame tigers, not to out-growl them.* Besides, if he were drawn into a growling contest or physical confrontation, the tiger would win every time.

Real tigers and our personal tigers are very similar. Taming your tigers is a mental ballet that involves *anticipating* your tigers' actions, knowing how and when to respond, and knowing what to pay no heed. You must remember, when *your* tigers growl at you, it is not personal. Just play your role: Keep a calm, professional attitude, and don't leave your feelings exposed where they will get clawed.

> Real tigers and our personal tigers are very similar. Taming your tigers is a mental ballet that involves anticipating your tigers' actions.

If anything goes wrong, such as the tiger acting nervous or aggressive, the tiger tamer immediately gives the tiger some space. You, too, should give *your* tigers the space they need by respecting their feelings and being mindful of what may be affecting their behavior.

Also, notice that the tiger tamer is not vindictive. He does not hold a few harmless growls against the tiger. He ignores the tiger's deeds when the tiger misbehaves, and he never hurts or punishes a tiger that does not do as directed. Further, he never intentionally provokes the animal, except as part of the act…strictly window dressing. Between acts, he makes every effort to win and hold the tiger's affection.

Like a tiger tamer, your approach and attitude will allow you to create a relationship in which your tigers want to please you.

Taming tigers - human or otherwise - is part of your job…and part of your life outside of work, too. Tackle the taming with a calm, matter-of-fact approach. Show no emotion except pleasant confidence. And *always* be professional: Play your role and keep personal feelings out of it. Don't try to out-roar your tigers. And *never* intentionally provoke them.

– Inspired by "Taming Lions," *original author unknown*

"Taming Tigers" - It's the wildest keynote on earth!

Chapter 2: Movie Magic

Hollywood Gone Wild!

*"My dreams were worth starving to death for. They were worth
dying for. I've died a million times for them... You have to
be willing to sacrifice in order to see your dreams
come true and then to help other people."*
-Dolly Parton, Entertainer

The lights dim in the theatre as the movie begins. It opens with a
wide, sweeping pan of an Asian jungle. Slowly, the camera zooms in
on a small patch of trees lying at the very edge of the jungle border.

As the camera focuses in closer, you see a solitary man coming into
view. He is facing away from the camera, scantily clad in tribal attire,
looking toward the inner depths of the forest. There is a strange
stillness in the misty air. He nervously peers back and forth, his
instincts sensing danger.

As the camera pulls back ever so slightly, you see the flicker of dusk
shining through the narrow, elongated grass and leaves, creating a
striated pattern of diminishing light against the dense foliage of the
jungle floor.

Dan Stockdale

You can barely make out the blending of the shadows against the beautifully striped coat of a Bengal tiger as she slowly stalks the villager for ambush. The light makes the distinction between foliage and foe barely discernible.

As the tiger prepares to pounce - the man, the prey, the hunted - begins to sweat profusely. He knows that someone, or something, has him in its sights, but he does not know who or what. For a brief instant, the tiger stands frozen, and then quickly lunges!

The jungle journeyman violently thrashes about on the ground in all-encompassing fear as 400 pounds of man-eating carnivore exhibits the task she lives for: to kill.

As the villager rolls in desperation onto his back, and the music builds to a crescendo, the tiger wields her fatal bite to the front of the man's neck.

Before you can see the physical effects of the ravaging attack, the scene quickly fades to a street scene of several thatched huts in a remote rural village in China. A man passes the camera on an ancient, rickety bicycle.

Several months before the completion of the final edit of the movie you are watching, the scene just described was being filmed, not on the continent of Asia but in the foothills of the Great Smoky Mountains. Of course, the attack scene was not real; it was all staged and carefully controlled. But how did they do it, exactly?

Filming the scene was not nearly as dramatic as it appeared on screen. The scenery was shot in the mountains, but the tiger was shot in front of a "green screen" in a studio in L.A., and the tiger was not actually attacking anyone. Ah, the mystique of Hollywood!

Want to know the inside scoop on how filmmakers get a tiger to give the impression of pouncing on its prey? Well, the tiger was simply asked to lie down, stand, and walk. Then, in a later take, the tiger was filmed, again in front of a green screen, jumping from one foliage covered pedestal to another. When the tiger "attacked" the villager and bit his neck, the tiger was actually standing over a costumed but familiar trainer, one she has known for years, drinking milk out of a baby bottle that the trainer was clandestinely holding beside his neck.

As soon as the director yelled "Cut!" the take was over, and the trainer hopped up, unscathed, and praising his feline "killer" for a killer performance. The obviously pleased tiger enjoyed her time on set, not to mention the tasty treats she received throughout the day for her performance.

With well-planned camera angles, fancy editing in post-production, and some of Hollywood's best scoring, you arrive at a scene with all the drama and realism of a vicious attack.

So, how difficult was it to get the tiger to do the series of behaviors that were shot in front of the green screen? Well, 'difficult' is probably the wrong word. It required many repetitions of several simple behaviors, learned over a series of months and pieced together to develop the movie sequence needed.

The scene also required significant planning; dozens of separate takes to get the exact angles, complex lighting and footage the director was looking for, not to mention several pounds of raw beef rewarded over a number of hours for each behavior.

Such is a day in the life of a Hollywood animal trainer and a working cat. It is very satisfying to a trainer, especially realizing how the audience will enjoy the finished product. But is it exciting and glamorous? As you can see, not so much, and you have not even heard about all the things trainers do when they're not training the animals to perform their behaviors!

Grrrrrr! – This is my mean look!

Chapter 3: Wild Thing!

A Tiger's Life in the Wild

*"What lies behind us and what lies before us are tiny matters,
compared to what lies within us."*
-Ralph Waldo Emerson

To understand the tigers we face in the jungle of business and life we must first look briefly at a tiger's life in the wild.

Baby tigers have been in the womb for around 103 days by the time they are delivered into this world. They arrive helpless and blind to the licks of a mother.

To be a wild tiger is to live a perilous life from the time you are born. Tigers eat their young! If a younger male tiger is successful in taking over a territory from a generally older, competing male, the new tiger will kill any young cubs so that he can immediately begin establishing his own genetic line. How's that for a happy childhood!? No crib and soft blankets here. At the expense of using a cliché, it *really* is a jungle out there!

After the new cubs are around two months of age the mother will begin taking them to the location of kills she has made. They learn the ropes quickly! By the age of six months she begins teaching them the fine are of stalking, hunting and killing prey. Cubs stay with their mother for fourteen to eighteen months of age or more before they venture out on their own to establish their territory.

Unlike lions who are pride animals, tigers are solitary. Tigers live by themselves, however, a male will generally have a large area that covers several females areas.

When full grown, tigers will reach eight to ten feet in length and they can weigh anywhere from 220 to 600 pounds. Tigers reach maturity at around three to four years old for females and about a year later for males (please, no wisecracks here!).

So, where do tigers live? They live in extremely varied climates from the reedbeds of Central Asia to the tropical rain forests in Southeast Asia to the mixed conifer-deciduous forests of the Russian Far East. Tigers indeed have adapted to extreme environments!

Tigers in the wild are skilled killers. Unlike lions and cheetahs who hunt in open areas with differing techniques, tigers us a "stalk and ambush" method of attack. The attack is swift and deadly.

Tigers too are man eaters. In the Sundarban Tiger Reserve tigers frequently attack the villagers. Human deaths occur frequently and without warning. Too, tigers attack people for three general reasons: 1) hunger, 2) fear, or 3) injury and old age. Regardless of the reason, the Sundarbans is not a place where you want to roam.

A tiger's life span in the wild is only around fifteen years, however, tigers in captivity generally live to be around 25 years old. The reason for the improved lifespan in captivity is the animal's immediate access to veterinary care as well as the absence of threats from other tigers.

A tiger's life is fraught with danger from beginning to end. Although they are an umbrella species – at the top of the food chain – they face many perils. Other tigers will attack and kill. Humans will attack and kill. Humans will encroach upon their habitat destroying their homes and the homes of the prey which the tigers feed upon. All of this danger results in a decreased genetic pool – never a good sign for an endangered species.

Even a tiger, the most majestic creature in the world, has it's challenges. It *really* is a jungle out there!

You never know what you will find sleeping in your hair when you wake up in the morning!

Chapter 4: The Making of a Tiger Tamer

Corporate Tiger Tamers & Exotic Animal Trainers

"Go confidently in the direction of your dreams!
Live the life you've imagined.
-Henry David Thoreau

Although there are some notable exceptions, like Mark Oliver Gebel, son of the great Ringling Brothers animal trainer Gunther Gebel Williams, most animal trainers are *made*, not *born*. And although it is admittedly a rare and exotic occupation, I entered it in a fairly conventional way.

I was not born to circus folk, nor am I a frustrated actor who would do anything to get my name in movie credits. Like many people, I have always loved animals, and for some reason I am especially drawn to big cats – tigers, specifically.

When I was 15 years old, I attained a summer job working at a small theme park in Tennessee. The park had its share of exotic animals, and I found myself caring for a herd of deer, three macaws, four dolphins, and twelve sea lions (but no partridge in a pear tree!). That summer, I knew I wanted to work with animals in some way for the rest of my life. We just connected.

Dan Stockdale

Now, I must tell you, most of us have a much sensationalized vision of what it must be like to work with animals. We see them onstage and on-screen, and they are clean, focused, and able to perform amazing behaviors. But what you see as an audience member is possibly *ten percent* of a trainer's life with an animal. The rest of the time, the trainer is scooping tiger dung, cutting up dead rats for raptors, and weighing fish for sea lions. Usually, it is a very smelly, dirty business.

But I also found it exhilarating, and I really felt I had found my calling. At the end of that summer, I went back to my family in Ohio, finished high school, and decided to get my degree in psychology so I could study behavior extensively.

For a few days in college, I had a memorable early "animal" training experience in a lab, trying to train meal worms to go towards a small, warm light in a simple T-shaped maze. I would put the mealworm at the base of the T, and then wait. And wait some more. Then I would nudge it a bit…and wait some more. Trust me; it was just as riveting as it sounds. And it did not work. Meal worms don't have the cognitive ability to learn the behavior. After all, they are worms. (And you thought *you* had some lame hobbies in college!) In retrospect, I am sure my parents must have been proud of their son!

The psychology major, however, was a perfect fit for me. I wanted to understand behavior and motivation, in humans and animals. But I was also enamored with business. So I ended up with a degree in psychology and a medley of other courses, many in business administration.

Then I was ready for some hands-on experience with my beloved tigers, I worked with a trainer who lived about an hour from me and had eight tigers on hand.

Later, I spent time at a few facilities in Florida. What struck me about the time I spent at each location was how each operated so differently. I thought that it would be, more or less, the same everywhere. But each facility was housing animals in different environments, for varying purposes, and with sundry philosophies. I observed that policies, procedures, attention to safety, training methodology, and almost every other aspect of care was somewhat different at each facility I visited. Sure, the basics were the same - clean, feed, and train - but there were differences in approach.

> What struck me about the time I spent at each [animal facility] was how each operated so differently.

Later, I met the folks at a ranch for working exotic animals in California. My first day with them found me sleepily shoveling elephant dung at 8 AM. As you might imagine, when an elephant goes, it goes A LOT! You shovel, and shovel, and shovel. In an hour, we filled up the entire bucket attached to the front end of a tractor.

Hey, this was Hollywood! Wasn't it supposed to be glamorous? Surely someone other than the *trainers* shoveled this stuff. Nope. That was our load to bear.

And it only got worse, because next I graduated to shoveling lion, tiger, and leopard feces.

After I discovered a tinge of blood on some tiger feces (When will I learn to keep my big mouth shut?) I was "lucky" enough to receive the distinct honor of checking one of the tigers for hemorrhoids.

You may ask, "How do you check a tiger for hemorrhoids?" And I can't resist answering, "Very carefully!"

It must not have been a great experience for the tiger either because she tried to urine spray me. Good thing I have quick reflexes! One of the most important rules of animal training is to never take your eyes off your tigers, as you will learn in this book, and I was mighty glad to know that tidbit of information that day!

Then it was on to the bears. You got it: *more shoveling.* But it was definitely worth it. For example, when we took the bears a bag of apples for breakfast, Bernard came up to the fence to lick my hand, his way of saying, "Thanks." That is a pretty amazing feeling most people don't have every day!

It Is a Jungle Out There, For All of Us

Does anything about my long days-of-shoveling remind you of coming into the office on a Monday morning? Many people probably view *your* job as a pretty cushy affair, especially if you are in management, but it is not always pleasant work, is it? You probably don't have to check your charges for hemorrhoids every week, but you may come in Monday with high expectations, only to find out about all of the "stuff" that has hit the fan over the weekend. Some of your employees may have been "sprayed" by an unhappy customer or two or are looking for someone to lash out at themselves. And before you know it, you are knee-deep in the sludge, drudge, and challenges of another work week.

Same thing at home, huh? Things can be rocking along pretty well, then, all of the sudden, issues arise with our spouse or children. Maybe your child fails a test at school, or worse yet, an entire subject or grade level. Maybe a spouse springs an unpleasant surprise on you ("That new Corvette just followed me home, dear!") Fill in here the less than pleasant realities of your own life. We all have them.

The Fruition of the Training Tigers Techniques (aka 3Ts)

While I was learning to train animals, I had to work in the world of humans, too, to put bread on my family's table. And from my many different experiences in business, as well as by learning to train animals, I began to draw parallels between the two. The positive reinforcement techniques I was learning with the animals seemed to apply to every element of my very diverse background in business administration, management, entrepreneurship, sales, and consulting. I have owned and/or operated businesses ranging from healthcare facilities to a concert promotion company, a continuing education firm, a real estate development firm, and my own consulting firm, which I opened in 1999.

What is more, I began to see how these ideas could work in relationships *outside* of work as well. Positive reinforcement, *the* central premise of *Taming Tigers*, applies equally to executives and their spouses, to sales professionals and their children. I call it the "Training Tigers Technique" or "3T." Once you identify your "tigers," you can apply these principles and techniques in your own situations and relationships, often getting the same excellent results animal trainers have with their animals. Of course, I realize humans aren't animals but the principles that motivate all of God's creatures can be very similar at times!

I have witnessed first-hand the *Taming Tigers* principles of positive reinforcement in a wide variety of business situations, and seen these ideas powerfully affect all kinds of business and personal relationships. Again and again, I have observed managers and entire organizations that strive to create an environment that focuses on the long term, who are sincerely concerned about their employees as individuals, and who are mature enough to resist the temptations of the short-term benefits earned by negative reinforcement. These individuals and organizations that apply positive reinforcement consistently excel and achieve long term success!

> Individuals and organizations that apply positive reinforcement consistently excel and achieve long term success!

The Alternative: Focusing on the Negative

Conversely, I constantly see organizations that incessantly focus on the negative; their expectations are unrealistically ever-rising in spite of stellar performance by their workers. The constant demand for more and more, without acknowledging currently splendid performance, can lead to quick turnover of individuals who are often very high achievers.

Such constant demands can frustrate even the best performers until they feel compelled to quit. Then the company's performance wanes, customers who have built a relationship with the former employee go elsewhere, a new person is recruited and hired, and the push is on to get the new employee's performance up to speed.

If they manage to get to par, in appreciation of their efforts, they are often pushed for more until *they* become frustrated and quit like their predecessors. As a result, the company's performance suffers, customers discover the competition, and the obvious solution is to recruit and hire someone new to get performance back up to par...You get the idea, right? It is a vicious cycle.

- It is a long-term, never-ending, self-perpetuating corporate nightmare.

- It inhibits companies from achieving their full potential.

- It spoils employee morale.

- It damages employees, their families, and their lives.

- It is uninformed, irresponsible management, and it is a discredit to shareholders whose investments would be much better served with a positive, proactive management approach.

Fortunately, in the animal world, the negative approach is not used by professional trainers. To begin with, who in their right mind is going to push around a 500 pound tiger? Moreover, the successes of the past several decades from the trainers who have adhered exclusively to positive reinforcement have shown that we receive far superior results than those who, a century ago, employed less constructive methods.

A former employee and friend of mine, Patsy, recently told me about the changes in an organization I used to manage. She is in sales and has achieved unprecedented success in her field through the relationships she has developed in her local community over the years. She is truly one in a million!

She already had twice the sales of her closest competitor. Now, she has doubled that number yet again. Incredible! Yet, instead of increasing her pay, giving her a bonus, honoring her performance with awards, and giving public acknowledgement, her supervisor at the corporate office is placing tremendous pressure on her to further increase her sales.

Now keep in mind, when she quadrupled sales, she added several *million* dollars of revenue to the organization's annual budget.

What is his motivation for the perpetual push? Of course it is the never-ending drive for higher numbers. But beyond that, I have to ask myself "What is he thinking?"

Why was she telling me her plight? Because she wants a reference letter; she is going to make a career change. And guess where her customers will go when she finds the right position? You guessed it: to the competition!

Can you imagine how a trained animal would feel in this environment? What about your own pet you have at home? What if you asked Fido to sit, and he did, then you yelled at him to do it faster? Then, you asked him to sit again, and he did it perfectly on cue. But instead of praising and rewarding him, you ignored him, or maybe even pushed him to do it even faster still! If I was Fido, I wouldn't be too happy. As a matter of fact, it would not surprise me if he bit your ankles!

Why, then would a manager take such a negative approach? If it is so bad, why does anyone ever practice it?

It depends. Sometimes management chooses this negative path because they lack education, management training or principled leadership.

Sometimes management lacks long term vision. Or trust. Or ethics. Or compassion for the human beings in the organization.

Apathy and a dysfunctional corporate culture can also be root causes of the generally subconscious choice to "go negative."

Regardless of the reason, if the problem is not identified, addressed, and resolved, the end result can be devastating to sales, profitability, shareholders' equity, and even to the individuals who practice negative reinforcement, not to mention those they practice it on.

With Patsy, when she leaves, the operating budget is going to be destroyed. Her resignation will have a major impact on many people. Some will likely lose their jobs because of decreased revenue.

If any of this sounds even remotely familiar, I have good news for you: There is hope! And the problem is *not* that difficult to fix. It simply takes focus and a willingness to accept that there *is* a better way.

Can 3Ts Work for You?

Even abused animals are trainable and able to perform. As a matter of fact, many of the animal performers you see at theme parks and in the movies are non-releasable animals that were rescued from natural or human-produced crises, or were subject to human imprinting.

This, however, is one of the areas where people and animals are different. Human intellect differentiates us from the animals, which will learn and perform behaviors even if they have endured very difficult circumstances. If you have or know a rescued dog or cat, for example, you know they can often bounce back pretty quickly, even from abuse, but usually people have a more difficult time.

What if you are only familiar with unconstructive models in both your personal and professional lives? Maybe, as a result, your personal relationships have never been strong, and your career has moved in fits and starts: even when you have been very successful, it hasn't lasted for long. Is it possible for *you* to re-train yourself and then apply positive principles to your business and personal relationships?

Will you eventually be able to make the positive choice? The answer is "Yes"!

Unfortunately, it is entirely possible to go through life without encountering much positive reinforcement, especially in the executive suite. I actually had a reporter contact me recently to ask why the C-Suite has become such a snake pit in recent years.

> You are capable of allowing a defining moment in your life – a conscious decision to change!

Of course, all of us can always choose the cooperative model, but the operative word is "choose." Even after a long history of negativity, if you are capable of allowing *a defining moment* in your life - a conscious decision to change – you can and must make the move to 3Ts.

There should never come a point where you simply *can't* implement a cooperative model that focuses on positive affirmation. Step back and look at what you have achieved in your organization and in your home under your current model, consider where it is inevitably taking you in the future, and commit to *choosing* to apply these techniques and principles, *starting today*.

It is *never* too late!

Performance Panacea?

3Ts aren't a wonder cure, but they work far more often than not. I have witnessed employees who were very poor performers, about to be terminated, when management paid attention and made modifications to the environment - their department, their hours, or the people they worked around or for – and suddenly, their negativity evaporated, simply because of a change in their surroundings. It may not always happen but the potential payoff is certainly worth giving 3Ts, the Tiger Taming Techniques, a shot.

Here is the challenging part: To be a tiger tamer, you have to be tough and sometimes brutally honest. Frankly, it can be extremely difficult. It takes more resolve, more self-control, and more self-discipline to maintain a positive approach when a "tiger" sits on the other side of your desk than it does to cave in to tradition and become defensive and assertive.

Achieving balance and building relationships is hard work and not for the faint of heart. 3Ts can be nerve-wracking at times. Results don't occur as quickly as with negative reinforcement, and it can be a test of resolve. But it's all worth it in the end.

Let's do a quick reality check: If they were to be *completely* honest, what would your employees, peers, fellow board members, or family members say about you, your relationships with them, and the challenges you face? If they could fairly critique your approach to life, what would they say?

Are you tough enough to look in the mirror?

Are you tough enough to face your tigers?

TIGER TALKING POINTS

1. What is the primary job of a trainer?

2. Do the Training Tigers Techniques work only in business or can they be applied to personal situations as well?

3. Training Tigers Techniques are founded upon what type of reinforcement?

4. What is the perpetual push?

5. Why does management so often choose a negative path?

A surprise visitor on stage at a "Taming Tigers" keynote!
This is a five foot long lizard!

Chapter 5: Jackpot!

The Payoff for Taming Your Tigers

"Leadership is ultimately about creating a way for people to contribute to making something extraordinary happen."
-Alan Keith, Lucas Digital

Every day, all of us encounter people at work, at home, or in the community who are difficult to deal with. Situations arise, too, that sometimes are only minor inconveniences but other times have the potential to be totally destructive, creating a huge detrimental impact on our lives.

How you react to and deal with the "savage beasts" you encounter in your adventure is crucial to your survival in the jungle of life.

In addition, as humans on this earth, I believe we have responsibilities:

- To make our world a positive place for those who share our lives, even briefly.

- To build up, not tear down.

- To look for the good in others and help them to achieve their full potential in a positive way.

We do ourselves and those around us a disservice when we fail to make our sphere a positive place for all whom we encounter.

Tiger trainers work hard every day to make the lives of the tigers in their care spectacular.

The *Taming Tigers* approach can, quite simply, make *your* world a more encouraging place. Following these principles and techniques of positive reinforcement will make you a better director, manager, worker, spouse, parent, son, daughter, and friend: a better *human*.

It will improve morale, create a more positive work and home environment, and increase the loyalty, trust, and respect you receive from those around you!

Think about it: Do *you* prefer to be around someone who is negative or someone who is positive, complimentary, and uplifting?

Or think about the best bosses or teachers you ever had: What was special about them? Why do they stand out in your mind? You may not remember a specific thing they ever said, but I bet you remember how they made you *feel*, don't you?

If you are like most people, the boss or teacher you are thinking about spent more time *building you up* than they did *beating you up* – right? Sure, they may have firmly, even sternly, addressed issues with you from time to time, but they probably didn't personally degrade you on a routine basis. They made you feel *valued*.

And let's take it a step further: Their approach to you made *you* think highly of *them*, didn't it? You were probably very loyal and would have readily defended them if the need had arisen. You also felt very comfortable in their presence and never felt as if they were out to get you, right?

If you were lucky enough to know someone like this, they were using some of the *Taming Tigers Techniques* I will reveal in this book, and they never even knew it! Who would have ever thought that Mr. McDonald in high school was actually a tiger tamer disguised as a teacher?!

3Ts Pay Off in Many Ways
By using 3Ts in your relationships and interactions with others, you will find that positive, successful people are drawn to you. As a leader, you will find that you can positively affect those in your tribe – those with whom you come in contact and those who observe your behavior.

When more positive people enter your tribe, more business comes your way... promotions, recognition, and reward come more quickly because others see you as effective.

Obviously, when more positive people enter your tribe, more business comes your way. So, in turn, promotions, recognition, and reward come more quickly because others see you as effective.

I bet you never thought that learning how animals are trained could benefit your bottom line, did you? But it can!

3Ts are the keys to improved relationships in work and in all of life. Your cooperative approach will let others know you can be trusted and that you are interested in what is good for them, not just what is good for "Number One."

Furthermore, this technique also will improve your relationship with yourself; how good will it feel for you to know that others believe you have their best interests at heart? There is no better feeling than *earning* the trust and respect of another person, or a tiger for that matter.

Dan Stockdale

Taming the Tiger of Turnover
In your career, you will find that the 3Ts make the office a more productive and pleasant place for everyone.

Is turnover a problem in your organization? Let's look at an example of how *Taming Tigers* can help, using some hard numbers.

I know one manager, Carol, who applied these principles and reduced her annual turnover rate to a respectable 12.5%, while another manager who chose not to take positive action had a turnover rate that ballooned to an annualized rate in excess of *90% per year*. As a result, he only lasted in his position for six months before he was offered "the opportunity to explore other career options." Taming your tigers pays!

Ideally, as you implement these ideas in your organization, others will see your success and will begin mirroring your leadership methods as *their* model for management within their specific work units too!

3Ts Save Time
If you are like many people, you may have forgotten how good it feels to take action that results in positive outcomes, but you *will* solve problems with these techniques.

If you've watched even a handful of nature shows, you may imagine that tigers are aggressive predators that never fail. You will be surprised to learn that tigers are successful only 5-10% of the time in their hunt for prey!

I guarantee, however, that you will experience a much higher success rate than tigers in the wild while achieving *your* goals by using the 3Ts.

3Ts are a time-saver, too. You can implement the techniques quickly. You will find that you don't meet with the resistance you may have encountered in the past when using other, less positive approaches to management and human relationships. You will then spend less time hashing out everyone's complaints and more time focusing on achieving *results*!

3Ts simply change the culture wherever they're implemented. The more problems you solve now, the fewer issues will crop up in the future, and the more time you will have to spend as you want: developing your best ideas, creating new and better products, and enjoying all of your relationships to the fullest!

The jungle of life may not become a perfectly groomed garden, exactly, but that's no fun anyway! Your jungle will, however, become easier to navigate, less treacherous, and more productive once cleared.

Still can't see the forest for the trees? Maybe your life feels like a jungle alright, but you know you're not some kind of animal! And you may not be too happy with me telling you that you are. In the next chapter, I'll define some terms and then we'll jump right into the *meat* of the matter: How can taming *your* tigers make all of this happen for *you*? Read on and see!

TIGER TALKING POINTS

1. What is our chief responsibility as an inhabitant of this earth?

2. What are the benefits of the Taming Tigers approach?

3. What is the key to success in life and work?

4. How often do tigers experience success in their hunting in the wild?

Taming Tigers

Dan Stockdale

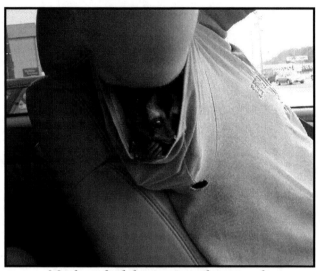

Monkeys find the craziest places to play
hide and go seek!
(please ignore the hole in my shirt!)

Chapter 6: Taking Care of Business

A Little Husbandry Before We Proceed

"Leading means you have to be a good example"
-Tom Brack, SmartTeam AG

Throughout this book, you will repeatedly read metaphors that draw parallels between animals and humans. Please understand that these are metaphors used to illustrate points and principles. It is not my intention to equate the huge span of human intelligence, accomplishments, and emotional range with animals, but merely to illustrate similarities.

Like us, animals are often social creatures with families, living in communities of others like themselves. Other animals, such as the tiger, are solitary in nature, only coming together for procreation or to mother young.

Like people, animals are intelligent, like to play, and, I believe, have feelings. But I am not equating "us" and "them" on every level.

I will ask you to keep your mind open to the idea that we do share *some* traits with animals. No, I'm not purporting evolution here. To the contrary I'm suggesting that each of us has the God-given ability to influence the behavior and traits of others. Chief among these traits is positive behavior in response to a particular type of leadership that we shall explore in this book.

Lazy Dogs, Sly Foxes, and Mean Old Buzzards

Throughout the book, I may attribute human characteristics and qualities to animals. This is known as *anthropomorphism*.

It is pretty common for us to think of non-humans and inanimate objects as having human qualities. Have you ever named a car? Or thought your household pet was smiling at you or possibly even plotting against you? That is anthropomorphism. For centuries, artists and writers have used anthropomorphized animals to tell their stories, endowing the animals with the human traits we associate with them. Think about Aesop's fables, George Orwell's *Animal Farm*, The Muppets, and Mickey Mouse and his pals; they are just a few.

I may anthropomorphize a bit myself for this same purpose to help you understand an analogy. It is a fun way to draw parallels.

Why Tigers?

This book is called *Taming Tigers*, but we will also talk about training other animals as well. Whether we are training tigers, monkeys, donkeys or eagles, the principles are all the same.

Animal trainers spend a lot of time and effort building trusting relationships with their animals. You should too when you are implementing these techniques in your business and personal life.

So I will use other animals from time to time to illustrate my ideas, but I believe tigers are the *best* metaphor for applying training principles to people. Why?

Working with tigers can be dangerous. Because of their wild instincts and sheer size and power, unlike many animals, tigers are capable of killing their trainers.

I don't mean that your accounting staff might turn on you with bared fangs – I hope not, anyway - but they might spin the numbers in a less than flattering way for your division, and in so doing, damage your perceived performance or ability within the organization. That's pretty dangerous, right?

Because that potential danger is there, tiger trainers spend a lot of time and effort building trusting relationships with their animals. You should, too, when you are implementing these techniques in your business and personal life. I will show you how to do that in the upcoming chapters.

The good news is that the Training Tigers Techniques are based upon positive reinforcement that is remarkably effective for tigers, enormous whales, and rebellious teenaged humans (who can sometimes seem more dangerous than a whole pod of killer whales, right?) as well as for the members of your work team. Even those angry, fang-baring accountants!

Why "Taming"?

TAMING
1. To force obedience; to domesticate
2. To suppress, restrain or subdue another's spirit
3. To control; command

TRAINING
1. To coach in or accustom to a mode of behavior or performance.
2. To make proficient with specialized instruction and practice.
3. To prepare physically, as with a regimen
4. To focus on or aim at (a goal, mark, target); to direct

The dictionary definitions above show us the semantic differences between the words *taming* and *training*. In this book, you may have noticed that I use the terms interchangeably, simply as a matter of literary convenience. However, technically, there is a difference in these two terms.

As you can see from the definitions, "taming" implies a *controlling* approach and connotes a negative experience. Forcing obedience, not unlike the process used to prepare young people for the armed forces, is distinctly frowned upon in the animal community. A professional trainer would never subdue a disobedient animal or attempt to break its spirit.

When I use the word *taming* in this book, I am simply implying that we need to get a grip on and control the obstacles we face. In no way, shape, or form am I implying that we should use a taming approach with either animals or humans.

Training, however, is a body of *methods, principles, and techniques* we use to achieve change: Sometimes we coach. Sometimes we reward. Sometimes we direct. Sometimes we redirect. Sometimes we shape behaviors. All of these training techniques are generally positive and are the "how" of achieving change.

In the next chapter, you'll get to do a little thinking about your own "tigers." Once you've learned who and what they are, you can begin to apply the Taming Tigers Techniques and principles to improve your professional and personal lives.

TIGER TALKING POINTS

1. What is anthropomorphism?

2. What do tiger trainers do to help counteract the potential danger?

Tigers are truly the most majestic creatures on earth!

Chapter 7: Safari Time!

Identifying the Tigers in <u>Your</u> Jungle

*"You have to believe in something yourself first,
before you can get others to believe."*
-Ashraf Seddeek, Oracle Corporation

> Identify your "tigers":
>
> What, or who, are
> your tigers?

The only time it is acceptable to "hunt" tigers is when you are hunting down the figurative tigers you face in your world. Real tigers have been hunted to near extinction because governments failed to keep an eye on their fragile populations. As we will continue to explore in more depth throughout the book, keeping your eye on *your* tigers is incredibly important, as you can probably imagine. No matter how great your relationship with an animal, even if you have raised it since birth, the animal is hard-wired to be a *wild* animal; it can and will attack. Never take your eyes off your tigers!

If you ever forget that fact and let down your guard, you can get bitten or mauled. Tigers are born killers! As beautiful as they are, they rest at the top of the food chain for a reason and must not be treated with apathy or ignorance.

Dan Stockdale

To fully implement the techniques and principles you'll learn in this book, you'll first need to determine who (or what) your personal tigers are. So, think about yourself for a moment:

What are the three biggest challenges you are facing right now?

- Do you have a large project that seems overwhelming?
- Do you have a micromanaging boss who is driving you nuts?
- Or a boss who seems to do little or nothing all day but chat with you and the other employees about golf?
- Is your "tiger" an unreliable co-worker or a team member who does not pull his or her share of the load?
- Is there a daily, weekly, or monthly report that just seems impossible to complete promptly?
- Are you wasting time, even falling behind in your work, because of seemingly endless, futile meetings?
- Maybe you are in sales, and you find it difficult to stay motivated to reach your quota.
- How about time management: Are you able to complete everything on your "to do" list each day with ease, or is there never enough time to get everything done?

What about your life outside work? What personal issues do you need to address? Or is everything sailing along perfectly?

- How about the kids and grandkids...any issues there?
- How is your relationship with your spouse or significant other?
- Do you feel fulfilled in your non-work roles? Spiritually? Emotionally?
- If they were *totally* honest, what would your friends say about you?

Additional questions to get you thinking about your unique challenges:

- Who or what is the biggest impediment to attaining your goals?
- What stands in the way of you receiving the award or other distinction you covet this year?
- What (or who) is standing in the way of your next promotion?
- What obstacle prevents adoption of your pet proposal?
- What are your financial goals? What is stopping you from attaining them?
- If you could change anything about your management or personal style, what would it be?

You have the idea now. Did your brainstorming give you an idea what or who *your* "tigers" are?

Keep Your Eye on Those Tigers...

In business, as in training animals, you don't want to ever take your eyes off your tiger. Now, your tiger need not be your *only* focus, but it had better be your *primary* focus, or you *will* get bitten. Only when you focus your primary attention on the issues of most concern will you have hope of achieving the best results.

Let's say you've identified a "tiger" as your organization's slumping revenue. Now you know what to focus on; don't take your eye off your revenue. If you operate an organization where revenues are decreasing, you can get so wrapped up in handling day-to-day operations, human resource concerns, and physical plant issues that, before you know it, you have taken your eye off your "tiger" - revenue - and it may sneak up on you and attack before you know it. And even if it doesn't, you aren't focusing fully to get income where you want it.

Your "tiger" may be a person, perhaps someone you perceive as a threat to you. Again, it may seem like a simple matter, but you want to keep your eye on that "tiger" and on what he or she is doing.

> Tigers can attack without notice. *Always* keep your eyes on your tigers!

Maybe a guy at work is friends with somebody on the Board of Directors, and that board member helped to secure his job. And now that guy has eyes for *your* job. I am not saying you need to waste time and energy in a worried, paranoid frenzy; you *do* need to be aware and perceptive, staying in tune with that person, and focusing on *your* priorities for the organization, not a rival's priorities for personal gain.

Keeping your eyes on your "tiger" is as simple as watching your back, or, better yet, *never* turning your back on your tigers.

So, who or what are *your* tigers? Now that you know, let's learn how to tame them!

TIGER TALKING POINTS

1. When is it okay to hunt tigers?

2. What are "tigers"?

3. When is it okay to take your eyes off of your tiger?

4. Who or what are your tigers?

Dan Stockdale

SECTION

II:

Discover the 7 Ancient Secrets of Taming Tigers

A tiger cub hangs out with Dan during a "Taming Tigers" keynote

Chapter 8: Tools & Techniques

There's More Than One Way to Skin a 'You-Know-What'!

"Challenge the process to the point of failure."
-Dick Nettell, Bank of America

In Chapter 6, I briefly discussed the difference between "taming" and "training," and explained how I use the terms interchangeably. Now, let's another look at this difference in greater depth.

TAMING
1. To force obedience; to domesticate
2. To suppress, restrain or subdue another's spirit
3. To control; command

TRAINING
1. To coach in or accustom to a mode of behavior or performance.
2. To make proficient with specialized instruction and practice.
3. To prepare physically, as with a regimen
4. To focus on or aim at (a goal, mark, target); to direct

Dan Stockdale

The dictionary definitions above show us the semantic differences between the words *taming* and *training*? In this book, you may have noticed that I use the terms interchangeably, simply as a matter of literary convenience. However, technically, there is a vast difference in these two terms.

As you can see from the definitions at the beginning of this chapter, "taming" implies a *controlling* approach and connotes a negative experience. Forcing obedience, not unlike the process used to prepare young people for the armed forces, is distinctly frowned upon in the animal community. A professional trainer would never subdue a disobedient animal or attempt to break its spirit.

When I use the word *taming* in this book, I am simply implying that we need to get a grip on and control the obstacles we face. In no way, shape, or form am I implying that we should use a taming approach with either animals or humans.

Training, however, is a body of *methods, principles, and techniques* we use to achieve change: Sometimes we coach. Sometimes we reward. Sometimes we direct. Sometimes we redirect. Sometimes we shape behaviors. All of these training techniques are generally positive and are the "how" of achieving change.

Taming vs. Training in the Real World
Let's look again at the difference between taming and training. Taming utilizes force, control, or demand. How many leaders have you seen who receive a position with even minimal power, and it goes straight to their ego?

Have you ever worked for or had a relationship with someone who tried to bend others to his or her will, either overtly or with passive-aggressive behaviors? They're not very pleasant to be around, are they?

What about in your neighborhood: does your community have a program for abused spouses? Chances are there are people who are living in your hometown, or possibly even on your own street, who are in bad relationships or who are the victims of those who try to control them.

Why do individuals seek to *tame* others? In all likelihood, in the past they have successfully reached their goals by using aggressive, sometimes hostile behavior. We continue to practice the approaches that have paid off for us before. Until one day, they stop paying off, and *then* what do we do?

Sometimes taming-types have superiors who see false value in the supposed "leadership" and "strength" being exhibited by unskilled, power-hungry managers, so they're continually promoted up through the ranks of the organization.

On the other hand, there are many examples of wildly successful organizations that use a relationship-based approach to management and leadership.

True leadership is getting people to *willingly* follow you, not *forcing* them to. Forcing a group of people or animals to go in your direction is called "herding." Herders *do* actually get the group to the destination, but they are certainly not leading, are they? Are you a herder or a leader?

> True leadership is getting people to willingly follow you. Herders try to forcefully direct others in the direction they want them to go.

Maybe you furtively relish your position and the power you have. But changing others' behavior through the methods you will learn in this book is *real* power. And it is real leadership!

Training versus taming: You have a choice. But if you want to *win*, you will go where the real strength is: *training*.

Dan Stockdale

It may help you to choose if you have a brief look at some training techniques at work in the animal and the human worlds, including real-life examples of how to implement them.

TIGER TALKING POINTS

1. Define "taming"? Who are some "tamers" you have known in your life?

2. Define "training"? Who are some "trainers" you have known in your life?

3. Which method is best at achieving long-term results? Why?

4. Why do people attempt to "tame" or dominate others?

5. How long should you work on building your relationships at work?

6. What is "herding"?

7. What is true leadership?

Dan Stockdale

Whips, Chairs, and Pedestals - The Tools of the Trade
For centuries, the props of tiger tamers were whips, chairs, and pedestals. However, in recent times, the "tools" we use with exotic animals are more closely related to *operant conditioning* than they are primordial devices. So what exactly is operant conditioning?

(Note from author: The next few pages are the most "academic" part of this book. The terms may seem a bit weighty, but I felt I should include them so that we all have in mind the same fundamental definitions. So, buckle up for a few minutes. And if you want to skip ahead past this section, I understand. I promise I will not give you an exam over the material!)

Operant Conditioning is the use of consequences to modify the frequency and type of voluntary behavior. Edward Thorndike was the first to extensively study the idea. He observed that cats placed in puzzle boxes took a long time to find their way out at first but over successive trials made fewer incorrect choices and experienced success more often and in less time.

Thorndike theorized that responses which produced *satisfying* consequences occurred more frequently because they were "stamped in" by the experience. Similarly, unsuccessful responses were "stamped out" and occurred less frequently. In short, some consequences *strengthened* behavior and some consequences *weakened* behavior.

B.F. Skinner developed Thorndike's ideas into a theory of operant conditioning involving reinforcement, punishment, and extinction.

- *Reinforcement* is a consequence that causes a behavior to occur with greater frequency.

- *Punishment* is a consequence that causes a behavior to occur with less frequency.

- *Extinction* is the lack of any consequence following a response. When a response produces neither favorable nor unfavorable consequences, it will occur with less frequency.

IMPORTANT: Note that people or animals are not reinforced, punished, or extinguished; the response is reinforced, punished, or extinguished.

Reinforcement and punishment may be either *positive* (introducing a stimulus to an organism's environment following a response) or *negative* (removing a stimulus from an organism's environment following a response).

In the context of operant conditioning, the terms "positive" and "negative" are not used in the popular sense of "good" and "bad." Instead, "positive" refers to *addition of reinforcement or punishment,* and "negative" refers to *subtraction of reinforcement or taking a reinforcement or punishment away.*

There are four possible actions in operant conditioning:

Positive Reinforcement happens when a behavior is followed by a pleasant stimulus to increase the frequency of that behavior. In Skinner's famous box experiment, a rat that performs a targeted behavior, such as pressing a lever, receives food or a sugar solution.

Negative Reinforcement occurs when a behavior is followed by the removal of an unpleasant, aversive stimulus in order to increase that behavior's frequency. In the Skinner box experiment, when the rat engaged in the target behavior, such as pressing a lever, it stopped the negative reinforcement, such as a noise continuously sounding inside the enclosure.

Positive Punishment arises when an aversive stimulus, such as introducing a loud noise, follows an undesired behavior, thus resulting in a decrease of the behavior.

Negative Punishment occurs when a favorable stimulus is removed – such as taking away a toy from a child who has exhibited an undesired behavior – in order to decrease in that behavior.

A few more operant conditioning terms:

- *Avoidance Learning* takes place when a behavior stops an unpleasant stimulus, such as shielding your eyes from the sun to avoid the punishment of having light in your eyes.

- *Extinction* happens when a previously reinforced behavior is no longer effective. In the Skinner box experiment, a rat might push a lever and receive a food pellet reward several times but then never receive a food pellet again upon pushing the lever. Eventually the rat would cease pushing the lever; the behavior would become extinct.

Operant Conditioning and Your Organization
How can you apply this information to your benefit?

Say you are chairman of a board that has a history of interpersonal conflicts. You lead the group to make a difficult decision that results in unity. You may, immediately after the decision, suggest that the board take a break or go out together for lunch – on your tab, of course - or plan a golf outing. You are following the positive *performance* with a positive *reinforcer* that the group will enjoy.

Now, keep in mind, one reinforcer will not establish behavior permanently. You need to continually watch for, or create, opportunities that are ripe for positive reinforcement.

An example of how *not* to do it would be to let the unanimous decision of the Board pass without comment, press forward through lunch without taking a break, insist on trudging through the afternoon's agenda without pause, and let things move back toward more adversity before adjourning for the day. That would be a prime example of *extinction*.

Patience, Young Tiger Tamer
As you will see, effective training involves exercising patience, so these techniques can be initially difficult to master because many of us seek instant results and immediate gratification.

We live in a society that encourages such impatience; we have instant email and attachments, fast food, TiVo, and on the spot access to information via the Internet. We are hooked on the quick fix, which accounts in part for our natural tendency to go more toward the punishment or negative reinforcement model, which can give the desired immediate result, though not the long-term, best outcome.

With any of the Training Tigers Techniques, the desired behavior may come in a few days, a few weeks, or even months. But the amount of time it takes to achieve the behaviors – to tame your tigers - is ultimately less important than attaining your goal.

A 3Ts Sampler
Here are a few simple examples of some training techniques used to teach animals behaviors and their equivalents in the human world. I will discuss these concepts in more detail in later chapters.

You'll probably notice that some of the techniques will be new to you, while with others, you will see how you have been using them to some degree throughout your career. The goal, however, is for you to gain an intuitive level of knowledge so that they become second nature. You can apply them *properly*, and get the results you want as quickly as possible, while still preserving the relationships involved.

Successive Approximation / Incremental Achievements
In animal training, successive approximation, also known as "shaping," is an essential training method, equivalent to teaching through "baby steps." For human training, I call it *incremental achievements*.

Think about trained dolphins at a marine animal park. How do they learn to leap so high out of the water and over a rope on cue? One way to do it is with successive approximation. Initially, the trainer takes a rope and lowers it to half the depth of the pool. If the dolphins swim *under* the rope, the dolphin does not get a fish. But when they swim *over* the rope, they *do* get a fish. Dolphins are smart animals, and hungry ones, so they will swim over the rope again and again to get a fish. *They are being rewarded for giving the trainer the desired behavior.*

Meanwhile, the trainer gradually cranks the rope up a few inches at a time. And as the dolphins swim *over* the rope, they learn that they will be rewarded, but when they swim *under* it, they will not.

It is important to note that *the dolphins are not punished* when they don't swim over the rope. They just don't receive any attention or reward. The trainer does not say, "Stupid dolphins. They will never learn this thing. Let's give up and go find *smarter* dolphins to train." Instead, dolphins and trainer persevere, even if it takes awhile, until the trainer achieves the behavior he or she seeks.

Increase sales and revenue! Raising the bar is an excellent method to enable your organization to see ever-increasing results! Oh yeah, and it works with dolphins too! Achieve maximum performance!

Soon, the rope is on the surface of the water. What are the dolphins going to do? If they swim under the rope, no fish. So they move their bodies up over the rope, and they get fish. Progress is noticed and rewarded, as the trainer, week by week and month by month, starts pulling the rope out of the water, inch by inch, until maximum performance is achieved.

Kind of lends a new meaning to the expression "raising the bar," now, doesn't it?

It works the same way with a tiger: if a trainer wants him to get on a seat, sit, then sit up, the trainer gets him to the seat first, sitting as a dog would. Then, to get him to rise up, the trainer places a chunk of meat on the end of a stick about an inch above his nose so he must raise his head and body up to get it. Gradually, the chunk of meat rises higher and higher until the tiger achieves the pose the director wants for that particular shot.

Incremental Achievements: Baby Steps to Your Success
Incremental achievement in your professional and personal life translates into small successes leading to the desired end result: raising the bar, raising the standard, and gradually taking achievable steps to reach an ultimate goal. You shape the desired behavior one step at a time.

Consider how these incremental achievement scenarios might work in *your* organization.

If you have a manager who is not turning in weekly reports on time you may..
.

1. Work with the manager to ensure that he knows how to create the reports.

2. Ensure that he knows when they are due.

3. Make sure the manager knows how to work the equipment necessary to deliver the reports - fax, email, or whatever system is used.

4. If the report is due on Tuesday of each week, call the manager on Friday of the week before to make sure

he is getting the information together. Then check back on Monday to see if he needs any additional help. Then check back on Tuesday morning just to see if there are any last minute details or questions. Continue this process for a week or two, then...

5. Call only on Friday and Tuesday. Continue this for a 3-4 weeks, then...

6. Call only on Tuesday. Continue this for 3-4 weeks, then...

7. Try not calling at all *for that purpose* but still call.

I used this technique with a manager who was having a difficult time with her weekly reports due to a combination of factors: She was insecure with the technology, had not ever had to complete weekly reports until she came to our company, and so forth. I patiently had to help her develop the skills and habit so that the reports became part of her routine. It took awhile, but then I began to see the results I sought.

Let's look at another common workplace issue and how incremental achievement techniques can work:

If you have employees who have difficulty arriving at work on time...

1. Make sure they know when they are scheduled to arrive. (Sounds foolish but you may be surprised!)

2. Make sure they know where the time clock is located (Again, may sound foolish, but you never know!)

3. Make sure they know how to use the time clock. (I know, I know. It really should not have to be this detailed, should it? But anyone who has managed employees for any length of time can relate examples of "Duh" events when employees *claimed*

ignorance of something that *anyone* would know
how to do in an effort to avoid punishment.)

4. If they are scheduled to arrive at 9:00 AM, but they
generally don't arrive until 9:20, praise them
sincerely when they make it in by 9:15, and so forth
until you have them arriving on time.

5. Figure out what motivates individual tardy employees,
then reward them accordingly when they show up to
work on time. Slowly, you can back off the
'Attaboys' until the behavior has become habit.
Mind you, it is going to take a while. And there may
be relapses.

When you're training using incremental achievement, realize that
you're trying to change a habit that has most likely developed over a
lifetime.

Does there ever come a time when you can stop? It depends – on how
well you have reinforced the behavior and how trainable the
employee is.

I have used this incremental achievement technique with employees
and have personally seen it work. As tempting as it may be to
negatively reinforce with punishment and write-ups and all of those
other quick-fix methods, give it a shot. You are very likely to be
pleasantly surprised. And, it certainly beats terminating an otherwise
outstanding performer and trying to find someone capable of filling
his or her shoes. It also beats tolerating the behavior from the star
performer and sending the wrong message to other employees.

Redirection / Fresh Focus
Redirection means refocusing attention. In this technique, the trainer
redirects the animal to another behavior that is incompatible with the
initial behavior it is presenting. For example, if one tiger is acting
aggressively toward another, the trainer could redirect the aggressor

to perform another behavior, such as sitting on a pedestal, and then reward *that* behavior.

When working with people, I call this technique *fresh focus*. When you encounter a situation where someone who is generally an asset to the team has lost focus on a vital task, you may want to use the fresh focus redirection technique.

It works like this: In some situations, you might not blame an employee for a problem but would instead redirect the blame to yourself, then redirect the employee to perform the correct way.

For example, if an individual was consistently preparing a document incorrectly, rather than blame him or her for being lazy, slow, or inattentive, you sincerely take the blame for not having made your instructions clear, then show in detail what was done incorrectly and how to do it right so the employee clearly understands. Finally, you express your trust that the employee will do the task correctly in the future and offer your on-going support.

Maybe you actually did make the instructions understandable or maybe you didn't; that's not the point. The point is to give the employee a chance to save face, even if it's at your expense. Your goal is to get the document prepared correctly, not to assign blame.

You may also use fresh focus when you notice someone who is concentrating too much time or energy in one area. When you redirect their attention, people will often realize on their own that they have been unintentionally overlooking something important. You need do no more than refocus them.

For example, if you notice that the COO has been spending most of her time working with Finance due to the upcoming release of the annual report, while other areas have suffered due to her inattention, a simple 5-second fresh focus question can be all it takes to get her back on track. Ask, "By the way, Lisa, how are things going in R&D with the case studies on the XYZ project?" to achieve the desired fresh focus behavior.

Dan Stockdale

Another way to use fresh focus to deal with undesirable behavior is by redirecting an individual's attention to another task. If Bob and George are a team working on a plumbing project, for example, and Bob notices George visiting with the carpenters instead of helping with the plumbing project, Bob could redirect George by asking him to go to the maintenance shop for a needed tool or by saying he needs a hand pulling some pipe through the wall. Simple example, huh? Sometimes, we over-complicate things when the answer is straightforward and right in front of our nose!

With a VP of Operations who is hanging out in Marketing for no apparent work-related reason, you may want to send him/her on site visits. That is the beauty of redirection: They can't hang out in Marketing if they are on the road!

With fresh focus, you accomplish your intention *positively* rather than punitively.

Extinction / The Magic of Vanishing Behavior
The extinction technique takes a behavior that has been previously learned and renders it "extinct"; it makes the learned behavior magically vanish into thin air!

> Now you see it! Now you don't! Extinction can be a good thing when you want to make a "behavior" go away!

For example, for one movie you may need to train a tiger to walk across the set and then jump *up* on a pedestal. A week later, for a music video, you may need to teach the animal to walk across the set and then walk *between* two pedestals. In this case, you need to cause the behavior of jumping up on the pedestal to go away or become extinct.

So, how do you get a previously learned behavior to go away? To get a learned response to go into extinction, simply quit reinforcing it.

For example, your darling teenager loves to see your response when he takes the opposite opinion of yours. He seems to live for the ensuing banter that inevitably follows as each party attempts to convince the other of the accuracy of their beliefs. To him, it is the sport of debate. In fact, his life's goal is to be an attorney, and he feels it his calling to practice on *you*. You, on the other hand, don't find it nearly as delightful. Nor do you find it intellectually stimulating. In fact, you find it downright annoying!

So, what is a parent to do? Well, first you need to recognize what the reinforcement is: It is the 'enjoyment' of arguing! So, what do you do? Take away the reinforcement, and you will find the behavior quickly becoming extinct. If you simply ignore the onslaught of comments intended to initiate the repartee, eventually the provoking comments will diminish, and with any luck at all, the behavior will become extinct over time.

Oops! Accidental Extinction
Let's take the concept of extinction to another level – the *accidental* extinction. You have probably inadvertently caused behavior to become extinct using this technique a number of times without even realizing it.

For example, you train your sales staff to perform a task, say, making 20 cold calls per day by phone. You tell them your expectation, and they meet it consistently. You assume that they have this habit down pat...and they do.

Then you decide you would like your sales staff to also begin filling orders, in addition to their regular duties, whenever someone in shipping can't make it into work. You have your sales staff take a day off from cold calling so that they can go to the shipping department to train. Then they go back to cold calling.

But three days later someone in shipping slips and falls and is ordered to take off work and receive physical therapy for the next six weeks.

Dan Stockdale

Well, the folks in sales know how to do the shipping; surely they can help "a few minutes a day." Before you know it, though, the duties in shipping have replaced your aforementioned priority of cold calling. Days go by without any cold calls being made, and before you know it, there is not much new business coming in. Cold calling has become extinct, entirely by accident, because the desired behavior was not reinforced when the new behavior was added.

So, how do you get the cold calling behavior back? Simply make it a renewed priority and positively reinforce it.

See, training your tigers is not that complex, now is it?

Chaining Individual Behaviors / Linked Learning
In chaining, trainers link a series of behaviors together in sequence with a reward at the end of the sequence. In general, you begin training a chain or series of behaviors by starting with the *last* behavior you want and then working backwards.

For example, say I want to train a cockatoo to fly onto the stage, then on cue, fly to someone in the audience, take a dollar from his or her hand, then fly back to me and drop it in my pocket on cue.

Easy enough.

The first thing I would do is teach the bird to stand on my arm

Then I would teach them to drop a piece of paper into my pocket.

Then I would train the cockatoo to fly from Point A (ultimately, a spot in the audience) to Point B (my arm) AND drop the piece of paper in my pocket. When I am teaching my avian friend the piece of "Point A to Point B", as part of the chaining, I would use incremental achievements and start with very short distances, a foot or two between the two points. Then, I would stretch it out another foot or two, then a bit more until I had the bird flying twenty, thirty or forty feet from Point A to Point B – all the while rewarding him for each success.

Can you see how we weave techniques together to achieve a chaining of numerous behaviors? You simply work backwards through the sequence. Of course, keep in mind that the end result does not occur overnight. It will likely take months of daily training for the entire sequence to come together to near-perfection.

When training humans, I call this technique *linked learning*. Let's look at an example in Marketing. You may be training a new graphic designer to put together a print ad for a national magazine. How does the ad come together? You could train the designer to start at the end result and work backwards.

What are the final dimensions of the ad? Well, they may have to go to the magazine's website and look for the needed information. Or they may have to place a call to find out the dimensions.

What is the purpose of the ad? What is the organization's goal in placing it? What are we trying to achieve? Sales? Applicants? Is it an informative ad or a persuasive sales piece?

Then the apprentice designer needs the content. Who is writing the copy? How much copy will fit in the allocated space?

What about graphics? Are we using stock photos or do we need a photographer to do some custom shots for us?

You are chaining a series of behaviors together to achieve the ultimate goal of a print ad design for a magazine. There are a lot of elements that have to be linked together in a relatively set sequence in order to achieve the desired outcome.

So now that you've seen a few of the techniques that can be used to train tigers, both the literal and figurative kind, let's delve a little deeper and look at the seven ancient secrets at the heart of *Taming*

Dan Stockdale

Tigers. By the time you've mastered all seven, you'll not only be taming the tigers in your life, you'll be handing out copies of *Taming Tigers* left and right, turning everyone you know into tiger tamers, too!

TIGER TALKING POINTS

1. As a society, why are we so inclined to use negative reinforcement techniques?

2. What are incremental achievements?

3. What does "raising the bar" mean to you?

4. What is the most effective way to "raise the bar," quickly or incrementally?

5. What is fresh focus?

6. How do you cause a behavior you don't like to vanish?

7. What is linked learning?

8. What is "Point A to Point B" training in the animal realm?

9. Is it possible for the Training Tigers Techniques to become second nature?

A cotton-top tamarin - another endangered species.
We <u>must</u> begin doing a better job as stewards of this earth.

Chapter 9: Taming Tigers Secret #1

Commitment

> *"It's amazing: once they get started, people always accomplish more than they originally thought they could."*
> *-Randy DuBois, Pro-Action Associates*

One of the most difficult aspects of learning to tame your tigers revolves around commitment. To see real results, you must commit on two levels to make the *Taming Tigers* approach work: First, you must commit to the *Taming Tigers process* and then to implementing its *principles*, one of which is…you guessed it: Commitment.

Confused yet? Let's break it down a little. If you have read this far in the book, you are presumably fully committed to the idea of implementing 3Ts to tame your own "tigers". That is step one.

Next, you must commit to applying the principles used to train real tigers to the "tigers" you have chosen as the ones in your life that need "taming."

Commitment to the Process
The notion of "commitment" can be a bit abstract, and means different things to different people. The way I see it, commitment is a

frame of mind, a starting point that determines the way you make choices.

For example, say you have an employee who comes up to you and says that he can't deliver a required report by the deadline you imposed because his son has a baseball game. If you have committed to attempt 3Ts, you can't follow your patterns from the past, which might have been to give the employee a blank stare that says, "So what? I couldn't possibly care less. Skip the game and do your work."

If you are committed to this new process, however, you will forego the stare-down and choose a different approach. Besides, imagine a real tiger trainer trying to intimidate or otherwise stare down a real tiger. Do you think the situation may get tense? Commitment will not allow you to follow the same intimidating methods you may have once used with your "tigers".

> You must commit 100% to the process of "Taming Tigers" or you will fail. "Taming Tigers" isn't so much a series of leadership techniques as it is a way of life!

Sure, you may have been reasonably successful in the past by being inconsiderate and tough, but your organization likely can't claim to be a "haven of happy employee relations" and "skyrocketing sales success" either. As a matter of fact, there may be some days where you feel lucky to keep pace and not lose ground.

Commitment, then, is *you* making a decision to give these techniques a try – knowing that you are not going to be perfect – and realizing that not being perfect is okay. You just pick up, correct what you can, move on, and do better next time.

So, are you committed to the process?

Lasting Commitment in the Animal World

With animals, the commitment shows in the care the trainer gives them. What you see onstage in a performing animal show or on film is a very small percentage of the animals' daily lives.

There are innumerable other aspects of caring for animals, known as husbandry, and many of them are not especially pretty, such as checking for hemorrhoids or blood in feces, shoveling dung, cutting up unsavories (to us, anyway) for feedings and so forth. These necessary if unpleasant tasks require commitment on the part of the trainer, every single day, day in and day out.

The pay-off for the trainer is in the enhanced bonding with the animal. When you are providing for the needs of an animal, you are in its presence, so it gets to know you and familiarity develops.

In the animal world, trainers working in zoos, parks, and circuses are very focused on enduring relationships, and the people who hire them understand this. So if during a tour, the show in Topeka does not sell out, management does not blame and fire the animal trainers for poor performance.

If you operate a zoo, and daily attendance does not hit 5,000 every day, you don't get rid of the sea lion trainers. Management in the animal industry focuses on the long-term; what can be accomplished in a year? Two years? What behaviors can we teach the animals that will improve our shows down the road?

Training in the animal world revolves around *lasting* commitments. When you take on the task of training an animal, you take it on for the long term. When you look at behaviors, everybody understands that, while you may *want* a certain behavior *today*, that is unlikely to happen. There is a *process* trainers must commit to and follow to get the desired behavior.

And remember: we are dealing with wild, unpredictable animals with differing personalities. We may *never* get the exact behavior we want from a particular animal. Trainers have to be committed to both the steps of that process and to the animal itself even when the animal doesn't perform perfectly!

Commitment to Your Tiger(s) for the Long-Term

The next aspect of commitment is committing to the "tiger" you are seeking to tame – with whomever or whatever you have chosen to use the 3Ts model. You will perhaps be relieved to know that I am not going to encourage you to check your employees for hemorrhoids or cut up their food for them, but there are parallels to this commitment in your life and in your organization. Let's be honest here: It's easy to support your sales staff when they're all serious contenders for Salesperson of the Year, but what about when they're going through a bad sales slump? Are you still committed to their long term success then? What are you doing to support them during the tough times?

Similarly, when employees have been with you for years, it is very easy to stand by them while they're your highest producers, but what about when they're going through personal struggles and their work begins to suffer, or when they're overwhelmed and find it difficult to arrive at work on time? Are you committed to being there for them during those times, as well?

As a tiger trainer, you can't just fire your tiger when things are not going well. You have a responsibility to the animal. For starters, where would fired tigers go!? And, who would be crazy enough to want to tell a tiger "You're fired!"? Even Donald Trump would shy away from that challenge!

Now you may be saying to yourself "Whoa! Hold on a minute! Surely you don't think I have to be committed to my staff when they're not performing! My employees need to be committed to *me* and to the *organization*, not the other way around!"

Today, many corporations, and frankly, our society as a whole, seem focused on the short-term, sometimes exclusively, as opposed to developing a long-term vision and committing to that vision. In general, we are more active, less focused, and less committed. And we move from place to place, job to job, and relationship to relationship when we are bored or unhappy.

This trend translates from the larger culture into our organizational cultures, which nowadays rarely treat people in a way that makes them want to stay for the long term. Management focuses on, "What did you do for me today? Yesterday was great, thanks. I appreciate that. But today's a new day. What did you do for me *today*?" without looking at the bigger picture, the longer-term.

In reality, if we create a culture where we are committed to the long-term – faults, differences, personality flaws, and all – we will see a far different reality than what exists today. Managers should be asking themselves, "Though less than perfect, what are my employees' strengths? How can I develop those strengths and mold each person to a position most beneficial to the organization?" When you commit to viewing your employees as human capital assets instead of short term liabilities, employees are happy and loyal and as a result your organization flourishes!

> Tiger trainers must be committed to their animals. Are you committed to your "tigers"?

Of course, being a leader sometimes means making tough decisions. Sometimes we *do* have to fire our tigers. But it should only occur after we have committed to and implemented 3Ts. Then, if the employee's performance still does not improve, it may be time to send them to a tiger refuge!

Trainers Strike a Balance
As we said, in the corporate world, we typically think in terms of "What can you do for me today?" Yes, today is *very* important, today's sales are *very* important, and if you are responsible for the circus's payroll, and it is due tomorrow, that show in Topeka today is *very* important. So you must determine where balance is achieved and

strike stability, blending the short term needs and the desire for long-term, continuing commitment.

Let's say you are a trainer and you have been given the task of training a tiger to jump up on a pedestal from the floor, through a ring of fire onto another pedestal, then through another ring covered in paper to another pedestal. Maybe management wants the behavior NOW because they have arranged with marketing to have a film crew come shoot the behavior for a spot they are producing that is supposed to begin airing next month.

What can you do?

You know that it is not in the animal's best interest to force the routine, so that is out of the question. Yet you know management's need for quality. And you also understand that if management does not keep the cash flowing, you have no paycheck. How can you achieve balance between the short-term needs and long-term commitment?

You may be able to meet both sets of needs by having the tiger learn its part in small pieces. Each piece could be filmed separately, at the tiger's comfort level and pace, then let post-production cut and splice to put the entire routine together. The animal is not pushed, so there is no pressure, yet management gets the footage they need as they attempt to steward the long-term needs of the organization.

So, not only are you fulfilling your ethical commitment to the animal by not pushing it, you are also satisfying the business relationship and commitment you have to your employer by enabling them to get the footage they need.

One quick aside about commitment: If attendance at the show is falling (and revenue has fallen with it), and a trainer doesn't receive a paycheck, the animals don't begin taking care of themselves. As a trainer, the animals come first and the trainer's responsibility is to the animals. It is not uncommon for animal people to work many hours *without pay*.

"Why?" you may ask. Because they are *committed*: to the process and to the animals. They realize that there is a bigger picture than tomorrow's paycheck. This is an example of *extreme* commitment and is virtually unheard of in corporate America! So, am I suggesting that you work for free? No, but I am suggesting that those who work with animals demonstrate phenomenal commitment that we can all learn from!

Behavior Breeds Behavior

The Golden Rule of Tiger Taming

One of the *Taming Tigers* concepts comes down to simple Golden Rule basics. In terms of animal training, if I enter an enclosure with a tiger–and it could be a very well-raised, well-mannered tiger–and I act aggressively toward him, how will he probably act in response? He is going to feel threatened! So, how is he going to react toward me? He would probably lay his ears down and hunker back a bit, preparing to lunge. Or he may make some other aggressive move to defend himself because he perceives me as a threat.

Let me assure you that I am guessing here, because I would *never* do this!

You can see this type of interaction with sibling tigers that live together. They can lie around for a while, then play and run for a time. But, especially as they age, come feeding time, any tiger will fiercely attack its brothers and sisters (or any other living thing) if they approach its food. The relationship does not matter at that level. If the tiger feels threatened – in this case because another animal tries to take its sustenance - you can bet the perceived threat will result in an equally severe response. Yes, behavior breeds behavior.

You can probably see, too, how behavior breeds behavior in business. Typically, people will take the path of least resistance. If you have a department where the manager or the director is disengaged, and they are not minding the details of their area, you will inevitably find complacent employees who lack focus and direction, just like the manager.

Similarly, if a manager is attuned to the details of his or her operation, you will find employees in that department who are detail-minded as well.

Though this is not a complex concept, you might be amazed at how frequently I have seen managers placed in positions that were not suited for their personality and management style; this always results in poor outcomes for operations and for the company as a whole. But even worse, the individuals who work under the mismatched manager never experience the self-fulfillment born of achieving the extraordinary, which they could attain were they in an environment where they could give their best.

Or, what about the manager who takes an aggressive posture with an employee who is frequently late for work? Yes, managers must facilitate disciplinary actions on occasion. But, if the manager holds a *personal* grudge against the employee as opposed to simply addressing the situation in a professional manner - and makes the disciplinary action a personal, hostile affair - the employee will probably become very defensive and react with the same amount of belligerence that he or she is handed.

You can't let inappropriate work behavior continue, and you may feel frustrated that nothing you have tried seems effective. But if you express that frustration personally or forcefully, you will likely see aggression returned in kind. Not only will the problem not be solved, the expression of hostilities is likely to continue to fester until you have an even bigger, potentially more dangerous problem to deal with. Yes, real tigers are dangerous and can cause harm. Too, the "tigers" we face in business can present just as much danger. Handle your "tigers" with care!

In business and in nature, you can't deny this simple truth: Behavior breeds behavior.

TIGER TALKING POINTS

1. What is the Golden Rule of Tiger Taming?

2. What does it mean?

3. How would you expect employees to act if they are working for a complacent manager?

Chapter 9: Taming Tigers Secret #1 (continued)

Commitment - Part 2: Committing to Culture Change

Creating a Team Commitment

Even if the change you are seeking in your organization is not a radical one, even if you are not coming from a negative method of operation in which you have been entrenched for years, you must be fully committed to working in this new process (or you are not going to be able to sell it to everyone else)? The work will be a lot easier if you don't go at it alone. Garner the support of others in order to make the process a success. The fact is, your personal commitment to the process will earn the commitment of others.

Watch any animal act, and you will quickly see that the person onstage is not a "one-man show." There will likely be a host of other individuals who have made the event possible, some who you can see and others who operate behind the scenes,. There are backup trainers and production assistants and vets and video directors and stagehands and park hosts; the list goes on and on. Without the *team*, the show *possibly* could go on, but it probably would not be nearly as safe or as well-produced.

You see, teamwork is as important in the animal world as it is in *your* world! Teamwork is an essential element in your decision to transform your relationships. For 3Ts to reach their fullest potential in your organization, begin by aligning yourself with those in your organization who are likely to "get it." They become part of your Taming Tigers team.

If other managers seem open to the process, talk with them, get their feedback on how to apply these principles, and ask them what could happen that might derail your efforts. Also, begin looking at your employees and support staff. Who is likely to buy in, and who is likely to fight it?

Negative naysayer's will fight the process and ultimately sabotage the team's efforts, intentionally or not. Give them an opportunity to be part of the team and its new efforts, but watch them carefully. Though I rarely advocate "shooting the tiger," negative naysayer's are like venomous snakes that will attempt to poison the team's efforts, sometimes fatally, and can be lethal to the life of the organization as a whole. So attempt to apply 3Ts to change their behavior, but if it does not change quickly, don't hesitate to remove them from the environment they seek to destroy.

Commit Sufficient Resources
If you are truly seeking to make systemic corporate culture change, you have to commit to this program as a continuing, ongoing process. To that end, you have to commit resources such as time, effort, money, and people to effectively pull it off. And the larger your organization, the more time, effort, and money it takes.

"How much?" you might ask. It depends. The time can be significant because this process takes education. The financial cost will be related to the time allocated and to purchasing training supplies and reinforcements. You cannot budget a concrete number of hours or dollars. It takes a review of your current situation and from there, you can develop budgets.

But it is worth it, as you know from experience if you have tried corporate trainings before *without* being fully committed to them. You may have gone for an inexpensive or insubstantial program, or a quick-fix process that did not require or encourage any follow-up once the facilitator left.

One of my biggest pet peeves occurs in organizations that have problems - with customer service, for example - so they agree to do a round of training with their customer service employees, for an hour or two…and that's the last the employees ever hear about it.

> If you want to achieve true corporate culture change you must commit time and resources. It is an on-going effort that must be consistently reinforced.

Everybody goes back to work. Supervisors get busy and forget to treat the employees like the internal customers that they are. Then, six months or a year later, management shakes their heads in bewilderment, wondering, "Why are our customer service scores still so bad? We did that training, didn't we?"

Carve it in stone: Without commitment and adequate resources for on-going training and follow-up – there will be no complete, systemic culture change.

It's Always About People, not Numbers
I realize that the idea of commitment can be difficult for many of us to reconcile with our entrenched ideas about business. It may seem a bit unwieldy for your taste. Many of us go into business in the first place because we believe it's supposed to be cut and dried - rational, not emotional. After all, our training and experiences have taught us that business is all about the numbers and structure and procedures and systems. No one ever mentioned "commitment" in our college micro- and macroeconomics, accounting, and marketing courses, did they? Remember though, numbers are simply a reflection of the relationships in an organization. They show us what is going on with the individuals in the company and their relationships with those who do business with it.

But times have changed, and progress has been made in many fields through an understanding of the necessity of recognizing that, like it or not, we are imperfect humans dealing with other imperfect humans, not humans dealing only with pie charts, budgets, and percentages.

Take doctors, for example. Two or three decades ago, many physicians seemed to have a difficult time realizing that the body they were treating contained an actual person. Some had little if any bedside manner, and many of them, especially the "old school" types, still don't.

But now medical schools actually train doctors to talk *with* their patients, not *at* them during diagnosis and treatment, and sometimes even to explore the healing possibilities in laughter, prayer, and positive thinking. Whether it is officially sanctioned by the AMA or not, many doctors now bring a positive component into their treatment, as well as saying, "We need to eradicate these cancer cells with chemo."

In this more holistic view of the practice of medicine, the doctor commits to working *with* the patient and dares to go to instinctive and emotional levels with them, not confining the relationship strictly to the body.

The *Taming Tigers* dynamic is similar, taking a holistic approach to management, not focusing just on the system or the process or the task at hand; it looks at the entire situation, the entire person who is performing the function, over a continuing period of time.

It comes back to commitment. As leaders we must be committed to the people in our tribe. We view them not as perfectly designed components in a machine, but rather, as whole individuals, imperfections and all. We must be committed to these imperfect individuals just as we expect them to be committed to our imperfect self.

Many of us have a deep sense of commitment to rescuing animals in shelters. Many times, we will actually look for the animal who we perceive to need the most help and that is the animal we will adopt. We accept the animal, imperfections and all, and commit to that animal. It's not a perfect world, nor is anyone – no, not even you and me – perfect. Accept the shortcomings and work with them to create something wonderful.

Imperfect. Holistic. Committed.

Dan Stockdale

NOTES

Taming Tigers

Dan Stockdale

Chapter 9: Taming Tigers Secret #1 (continued)

Commitment - Part 3: Commitment Creates Connection

In the business world, we can be so driven to achieve results that we forget that *people* achieve those results for us. People and animals both respond better when they feel a connection. And connection is more than mere chemistry; it's about commitment.

If I walked into your house and tried to get your dog to shake hands and roll over, for example, he might not perform very well because I have no connection with him. He is likely to think, "Who is this guy and why should I listen to him? I think I'd just as soon bite him!" But if I commit to spending a little bit of time connecting with him, and I have the right treats...

With people, your interest and attention is the "treat," the motivator. You may be surprised to find that just a little bit of interest in others goes a long way. When someone pulls up next to you in the parking lot, for example, make a little connection: "I saw your new car. That's really great-looking. How do you like it? When did you get it?" However you make the connection, you are indicating your interest and commitment and laying the groundwork for working with this person. Over time, you will see the results.

I am not saying that your commitment here needs to be the sort of commitment you have made to a spouse or children or to others with whom you have intimate relationships or friendships. You don't need to be willing to take a bullet for anyone, or even want to have lunch with them, in order to make this process work.

Dan Stockdale

I understand that some in senior management can't or simply don't want to "hang out" with their organization's janitors or administrative assistants, and that is fine. However, it will not kill you to make a commitment to being reasonably friendly with individuals at lower levels of the organization. And small efforts aimed at connection will actually accelerate positive results and even have positive impact on your bottom line!

For example, if you have an issue with marketing – say they are not producing the type of material that can effectively sell your product - it would behoove you to venture into the marketing department and say hello every once in a while. You are not trying to make them feel intimidated or manipulated, but are instead visiting to show your commitment and support, indicating a sincere interest in what is going on, and making yourself available if you are needed.

Commit to Letting Down Your Guard
You may not have allowed friendships or even friendliness to evolve in the workplace because you believe you must keep your guard up at all times against potential attacks or even the perception of weakness. But a willingness to be *appropriately* vulnerable is part of the commitment you must make for 3Ts to work.

When trainers walk into an enclosure full of tigers, they necessarily let down their physical guard. They are always aware of their surroundings and take measures to be adequately protected – they never walk in naked, covered in *eau de filet mignon* – but they know they must remain open to connection and contact.

Wise trainers know that they are letting down the physical guard when they walk into the enclosure. It is a conscious decision that is made in a controlled environment, by professionals who have thought out the options in their mind and have planned for the worst-case scenario.

In the business world, you have to be willing to do the same thing. I'm not saying that you must be weak, by any means, but you must have the self-confidence to be *honest and open*, even when doing so may expose you or your weaknesses – and "Yes", it's okay to admit we have weaknesses – we all do.

There are various types of contact that trainers use with their animals:

- Free Contact
- Protected Contact
- No Contact

For instance, when the new policy and procedure you developed isn't working when it's put into practice on the assembly line floor, be candid with yourself, the staff, and even your boss. Don't go down in the annals of grand self-delusion by trying to convince everyone that it will work if they "stay the course."

Generally speaking, you will be respected more for letting your guard down and being honest about a *faux pas*, than if you staunchly support your original position. You see, you are actually in a position of strength when you're confident enough to expose some weakness.

Then, the next time you try to implement change, employees are likely to give it their best shot because they know that you don't tolerate a bad policy, even when it's your own.

Gauging Your Commitment
Animals are not necessarily committed initially to their trainers, but their trainers have to be committed to the animals. In time, however, animals will often develop familiarity and preferences for certain individual trainers.

Young cubs may not realize with precise understanding who each person is that is providing care for them at a young age, but they feel the commit

In human relationships, though, it is helpful if commitment is *mutual*. Of course, you can't force anyone to be committed if they don't want to be. It will, however, make your job a lot easier if you can find like-minded individuals within the organization who have the same philosophical bent and willingness to try to change behaviors with 3Ts. And don't be impatient: Remember, just like with animals, commitment can take time.

Maybe you aren't supervising anyone. So what's your commitment to your *boss*? What is your commitment to your *organization*? To your *family*? To your *community*? It's not uncommon to find employees who say, "Oh, yes, I'm loyal to my boss and the company," yet if you listen in on the break room banter, you hear quite a different story.

Maybe you tell anyone who will listen that your greatest commitment and first priority is your family. But when Junior has a baseball game, you can be found working overtime in the office. Granted, things come up occasionally that prevent even the most committed parents from being at every event. However, the telltale sign that your commitment is shallow is when you *could* attend, but, more often than not, find seemingly valid reasons not to.

Adopting this principle – really committing to it – means you'll have to do some soul-searching to determine how committed you are to achieving positive change in yourself and the behavior of others. It's okay if you haven't been in the past but do you feel ready to be committed now and in the future?

Commit to a Tiger Taming Plan
Practically every American commits to some goal on January 1st - losing weight, stopping smoking, exercising more - and by February 1st, most of us are back to "normal," in spite of our good intentions. We break resolutions because of a combination of unrealistic goals, a lack of commitment, and not having the tools and support necessary to help us reach the goals we committed to in the first place. No matter how sincere our commitment, we can't reach goals unless all of these elements are in place.

When you have determined your level of commitment, you must create a Tiger Taming Plan to achieve goals in relation to your particular "tiger." Your "tiger" could be a person, or it could be an issue, say, finances, but you must first be clear with yourself about what type of behavior you want to achieve with your "tiger." Consider what obstacles you have to overcome in order to attain your goals.

No matter how fired up you get about this process, strive to ensure that you set goals that are realistic and attainable. If your tiger is substantial credit card debt, and your goal is to eliminate it in one month, or even in one year, your goal *may* be unrealistic, and all the commitment in the world will not help you achieve it.

You will quickly grow discouraged and then feel guilty and frustrated that your commitment was not enough to carry you through to success.

Achieve Your Goals with 3Ts - Personal Goals

How can an animal training technique help us reach our personal and professional goals? Remember the technique called "successive approximation" that I told you about with the dolphins? Successive approximation is, in layman's terms, taking baby steps, and it is an excellent technique to learn for achieving the realistic goals you commit to.

For example, if a personal "tiger" is too much weight, "losing 50 pounds" in a month is not achievable, but "losing 50 pounds" in a year *can* be achieved. If that is your goal, you reach it by taking small steps, concerning yourself not with the big picture – you are already committed to that – but with each step, which in this case is each meal and being successful at planning and consuming what will ultimately help you reach that goal.

Give yourself a break, too; none of us is perfect. You will not eat perfect amounts of just the right foods every single meal, every single day. One way to help maintain your commitment is to not beat yourself up on those occasions when you overindulge.

Dan Stockdale

Now, that being said, you may be thinking "That's my kind of diet! I am allowed to fall off the wagon all I want to!" Wrong! This is not a platform to give the illusion of success when you're actually failing. It's simply a matter of not expecting yourself to be perfect.

In the animal world, if an animal has a weight issue it is caught early and addressed in small, simple, daily diet changes. For example, in the past I volunteered for a non-profit association that cared for birds of prey. Every bird, whether it was a screech owl, a red tailed hawk, or a bald eagle, was weighed daily. Any deviation in weight that may have been caused by the weather, their activity level, or other factors was immediately addressed by adjusting their diet that very day.

Achieve Your Goals with 3Ts - Professional Goals
Let's look at another example, this time in the workplace. Say you're the VP of Human Resources of a large commercial construction company, and you receive significant pressure from the COO because workers' compensation expenses are spiraling upward. How would you go about taming the tiger of workers' compensation costs?

A good first step would be to perform an initial analysis of the problem. What injuries are you experiencing? What part of the body is most frequently being injured? Backs? Commit to the process of discovering the root of the problem.
Under what circumstances do the injuries occur? Lifting? Turning? Carrying large objects or large tools?

When do the injuries occur? Early in the morning? After lunch? At the end of the workday? Commit to the process of discovering any trends.

What other commonalities do you see? Talk to the workers. Talk to their peers. Talk to the on-site managers. Commit to gaining as much knowledge as possible about your "tiger" of workers' compensation.

Then, begin thinking of solutions. Develop training programs. Implement new policies and procedures. Commit to the solution.

Now you have the opportunity to implement your tiger taming plan. Here is how you might use a successive approximation approach to accomplish your goal to lower workers' compensation expense:

- Step One: Take the research and develop an education session that explains why there have been accidents and what preventative measures could be taken to avoid the incidents in the future.

- Step Two: Schedule all employees for a time to attend the education session.

- Step Three: Provide additional safety equipment at the job site.

- Step Four: Train worker's on use of the new safety equipment.

- Step Five: Implement a measuring system for ongoing monitoring of employee incidents.

- Step Six: Initiate supervisor safety rounds so that managers are conducting routine safety checks throughout the day, and so forth.

> Safety is a paramount concern when working with any type of exotic animal. Trainers must be cognizant of safety at all times.

You've got the idea! You're just taking small, incremental steps toward achieving your ultimate goal of reducing or eliminating employee incidents. By committing to the process and implementing 3Ts, you quickly and methodically gain control over one of the "tigers" that lurks in your daily jungle.

Speaking of safety, as you may imagine, safety is a paramount concern when working with any type of exotic animal. Just like the construction workers mentioned in the above example we too as trainers must be cognizant of safety at all times. No just our safety as trainers but also the safety of the public and the safety of the animals.

Indeed, accidents do happen in all lines of work. Inevitably, whether its on a construction site or a slip and fall on the marble floor of a hotel lobby, the accident can likely be attributed to failure to follow the rules or carelessness. Whether you're the CEO of a truck driver, you need to be a leader with an eye towards safety and providing a safe environment in which others can work.

When accidents occur, we often see additional rules and regulations rear their head. Sometimes they are needed; frequently they are not. Often, what is *really* needed is additional training and reinforcement of existing protocols.

Commit to your tigers. Commit to safety. By doing so you will show that you care about your relationship with others.

NOTES

Dan Stockdale

Dan in California with Nellie

Chapter 10: Taming Tigers Secret #2

Relationship

"Support others, and they are more likely to support you."
-Marianne Hane, Applied Biosystems

The same training techniques that motivate animals also motivate people. You may try, but you can't truly *control* exotic animals *or* people; however, you *can motivate* animals and people to achieve the behavior you want from them.

Yelling, threatening, punishment and other negative behaviors won't give you the results you seek in the long-term. For enduring, positive results from your "tigers," you must develop relationships like trainers have with their animals.

Relationship is at the heart of the Taming Tigers approach. The best, most productive relationships, between animals and their trainers and between humans – inside the workplace and outside of it – are based on trust, empathy, respect, and a willingness to meet each others needs.

Dan Stockdale

Relationships with Animals and People Requires Grit
Stepping into an enclosure with a wild animal requires the *courage to be vulnerable*. Among those who work with animals, the heroes are not those who attack before they are attacked or who impose their will on animals; they truly revere those who have the ability to develop a relationship with animals: the boldness to learn, to trust, and to empathize to take the time to get to know each individual animal.

With animals, openness and empathy require courage. It's the same way with humans: employees or superiors, friends, foes, or family. You have to be present, understanding, and willing to be somewhat exposed in order to get the results you desire. It takes far more guts to open up to your staff and *sincerely* ask for their input, than it does to bark out orders. In other words, risk-taking is about much more than dropping a bundle of money on an unwieldy, unknown stock. It is about being brave enough to be vulnerable.

The notion of relationship can be inherently frightening to many of us, especially those of us who pride ourselves on being hard-charging business professionals. The very word "relationship" may conjure images of romance before revenue, and even those with a more sophisticated understanding of the term may feel unwilling or unable to communicate, commit, and do what is necessary to make relationships work outside of the personal sphere.

> The notion of relationship can be inherently frightening to many of us.

Even in business, relationships matter. Much as you might wish for business to be strictly about processes and rational, intellectual exercises, it's not. People with all their many and varied personalities and strengths and weaknesses, require you to exercise great bravery in ways you may not have considered before.

Free Versus Protected Interaction with Your Tigers
In animal training, "free contact" is hands-on; trainers interact with a tiger with no barrier between them and the animal. This is the most dangerous and intense type of training possible. It requires constant vigilance and adherence to training and safety protocols.

With "protected contact," though, a barrier such as a fence, or sometimes two fences, keeps the trainer protected from the animal while training. In a protected environment, training the animal is more difficult because there is less of a relationship, less contact, and obviously more limited interaction.

"No contact" is just what it sounds like: no contact between trainer and animal. No contact is used with animals that are going to be released into their natural habitat or for animals who are simply too dangerous for no contact or protected contact.

These three types of training offer good analogies to our relationships, both in and out of the workplace. Typically, we erect barriers or "walls" in our relationships that seem to serve as protection against the pain that may accompany negative behavior. If we encounter difficulties in our relationships or a relationship ends, we may feel as if we have protected ourselves, avoiding the "dangerous" feelings that can accompany its end. However, these barriers to potential "negative" feelings make it more difficult for us to develop closeness and trust in our relationships. We have to be "exposed," in free contact, in order to fully experience the positive feelings that a meaningful relationship provides.

While we potentially must take much greater personal and professional risks when we operate in a "free contact" mode, we also experience far greater rewards.

I recall the first time I was in a free contact situation with a tiger. As you may imagine, I was a bit apprehensive. I remember looking at him, seeing his *massive* size, and wondering what in the world I was doing there.

Dan Stockdale

When you are totally outsized, completely at the mercy of an animal who can take you down in a split second, you sharpen your senses – quickly! I recall thinking about the power and muscle he had at his disposal. Yet, he was sizing me up just as I was he. Yes, free contact can be very exhilarating!

I once had a client who was an area supervisor for several business locations. Charlie was a control-oriented person and wanted to make all decisions on his own, with no input from anyone. When he contracted with me to look at his business units, I found that he was hiring the wrong key managers, with the wrong skill sets and inadequate experience. I had been hired to perform a function and tell him the truth about what I saw, so I did.

What happened? You guessed it: He did not want my input either, even though he was paying me for my opinion. As I got to know Charlie, I found that he'd had some very difficult circumstances in his personal life many years prior. Those experiences had caused him to go into a "protected contact" mode with *everyone* he came in contact with.

Over a period of about a year, whenever he wanted to hire someone, I would research their background and look at Charlie's needs. On several occasions, I would recommend he keep looking. He would hire them anyhow. I would move on to another consulting job. He would call me 6 weeks later, asking me to come help him again because he was getting ready to terminate the person he had just hired.

We would find someone else he wanted to hire. I would research their background and look at the business unit and its needs. If the candidate was not qualified, I would recommend he keep looking since the person he wanted did not meet the qualifications. He would hire them anyhow. I would move on to another consulting job. He would call me 6-8 weeks later and ask me to come help him again because he was getting ready to terminate the person he had just hired.

This cycle went on for almost a year. It was, frankly, insane, and it caused major upheavals in the business operation as well as costing him tens of thousands of dollars in fees.

Finally, Charlie allowed me to operate in 'free contact' with him. We researched and hired. The manager stayed for years! I did not do anything magical, but I did finally find a way for Charlie to trust me, to let me move from protected contact to free contact, and this move benefited Charlie, the business, and the employees.

You must give the decision to operate free or protected a lot of thought. Are *you* willing to assume the risks …and reap the rewards?

Is There an Elephant in the Room?: Gain Credibility by Acknowledging Reality
Am I really advocating that you expose your deepest personal vulnerabilities to people you have to work with day in and day out? Absolutely not. But in business relationships, if you are not currently experiencing unqualified success – or are maybe even careening down what is clearly the wrong path in your jungle – you must be willing to acknowledge where you have weaknesses, what you are potentially doing wrong, and what needs to change to put you back on the right path.

> To catapult your "Tiger Taming" success, acknowledge the elephants in the room!

Think about it: Have you ever had a boss who was clearly in the wrong, being eaten alive by the "tiger" in his life, yet he would not allow himself to acknowledge it, let alone make a sincere effort to eliminate the problem? That "tiger" was actually the preverbal elephant in the room that no one would acknowledge.

You may not realize how many others can see what you can't or won't see. And it instantly enhances your credibility to acknowledge what is already crystal clear to others. Just because *you* are not acknowledging the 4-ton elephant in the room does not mean it's not

Dan Stockdale

there. It just means you're not acknowledging it. So the other people in the room with you, and that elephant, will not take seriously any attempts to conduct business *around* the elephant until you make it clear that you understand that it's there.

If that elephant is past mismanagement or poor approaches to situations, you will have to acknowledge these issues and show that you are seeking to implement a better way of managing. When those in your tribe see that you are willing to be realistic, open, and honest, it builds trust. This trust then further improves relationships.

If a salesman works for a widget company, and the widgets are defective, do you think it builds business if customers call to voice their complaints, and he denies the defect? Or worse, tells customers that they're using the product incorrectly?

Wouldn't it be better for him to acknowledge the defect, offer to replace the widget (or even refund the money), and send a personal note of apology after correcting the situation?

Acknowledge the elephants – and the defective widgets – and make the situation right, do something extra, build your credibility, and enhance your relationships!

By the way, not acknowledging an elephant can have disastrous results. Have I ever told you about the time I was walking behind an elephant that had diarrhea? …on second thought, never mind!

Positive Reinforcement for Negative Relationships
So what's wrong with running your department with an iron fist?

What's the problem with "watching your back" around your co-workers or even taking pop shots at them, especially when it has the potential to further *your* career? Besides, it's about time you released the tiger within, right!?

The more you tear down your peers, the better *you* look, right? That's just being smart.

If what you're doing works for you, why should you want to stop? The truth is, very often we can achieve extremely good results with negative behavior, so, ironically, we're positively enforced for being negative.

Here's an example of how that works: Large organizations tend toward the negative model because of potential legal ramifications. If you must deal with a habitually late employee, for example, you are very rarely going to have your Human Resources manager or your company's legal counsel or risk manager say, "Well, shucks, let's not focus on the problem here; we don't want to appear too aggressive. Why don't we reward him for his *good* behavior?"

What you will hear is, "Do you have your documentation in order? Have you given him a verbal warning? Is it documented? Have you given him his first written warning?" and so forth. From HR's perspective, documenting the negative is essential if they have to fight an unemployment claim or discrimination suit. They want the records to back up what a poor employee this person was.

What's more, in this situation, *you* are being positively reinforced for punishing the employee. If you take all the steps Human Resources advises – give all the warnings, both verbal and written - and it culminates in the employee's suspension and termination, Human Resources will get the file and see that you followed the proper steps, to the letter.

So what does *your* evaluation say? "Excellent file. Perfect paperwork. Detail-oriented. Does a great job!"

You are now one of HR's favorite managers, because they are accustomed to getting incomplete files and fighting with attorneys because other managers in the organization have not been nearly as thorough with their documentation.

Dan Stockdale

Let's look at another example. Say you are a sales manager. Sales are down, and you respond by berating and threatening your sales force. Scared for their jobs, suddenly they begin making more sales contacts. Sales jump, you look great – no matter how much your sales people may resent or fear you. The numbers trend north, the VP of Sales calls the sales manager to congratulate her on a job well done, and you have just been positively reinforced for using fear of punishment, a negative technique.

So the sales manager who gets better sales out of his or her people by bullying and intimidation (and/or other negative techniques) may continue to be successful. After all, a manager who is always increasing sales is doing what he or she is *supposed* to, right?

The corporate office is happy because the numbers are up, and therefore the shareholders are happy. Shareholder happiness leads to boosted stock prices. And if the stock price increases, we are *all* happy and all is right in the world! Right?

Wrong!

Intimidated Tigers and The High Price of Negative Relationships
The intimidated sales people eventually get fed up and fight back. Sometimes our subordinates fight back with their feet; they walk. This high turnover affects the bottom line, long-term. Those who don't leave lack morale; there's not a shred of job satisfaction or individual happiness to be found. Training costs for each new crop of producers escalate. Eventually, *somebody* goes to the CEO and says, "The reason turnover is so high and sales are plummeting in our department is because our supervisor is on a power trip."

While theoretically managers can operate successfully under a punishment or negative reinforcement model, they will eventually encounter significant consequences.

Fortunately, I have never seen a professional animal trainer or facility personnel mistreat their animals. I can't count, however, the times I have seen managers bungle relationships with employees through their lackluster or abusive management style.

Also, managers and organizations that accept the negative relationships as normal and appropriate tend to be ethically lacking. We all have a moral obligation to make our tribe a *better* place. Just as animal trainers have a moral and societal obligation to care for their charges in an appropriate manner, we, too, have an obligation to ethically lead those under our stewardship.

Negative relationships are also problematic, even dangerous, because while they may be working for you now, you can't count on them working forever. If you treat your tigers negatively, it may work for a while – maybe even months or years. However, there *will* come a day when you'll regret your actions: when your tigers realize that they have the power to take you down and dominate you. And they will if the opportunity arises. They will eat you alive.

Negative relationships may be working fine for you in one aspect of your life, say in your business, but not in another, such as with your family. It may come as no surprise that an individual who approaches work relationships from a negative standpoint will generally use the same tactics in personal relationships. Rarely are people utterly unconstructive in one realm of their lives while maintaining a completely positive approach in the others.

> Caution: Negative relationships can be problematic – even dangerous!

And in those personal relationships, if you only practice negative reinforcement, you are ultimately going to end up alienating your family, friends, and others in your world. It will be difficult, if not impossible, for you to have close relationships if your operating principle is wholly or mostly disapproving . Even if there is a hint of a relationship there, it most likely will not be a productive, satisfying, positive one.

Dan Stockdale

Extreme Predators – When Tigers Turn
Imagine for a moment that you are a tiger trainer. Your job is to walk into an enclosure with five tigers and train each of them to sit on a pedestal. Most of us have seen this done in circus acts before. It seems pretty simple, doesn't it? All you have to do is get them to walk over to the pedestal, hop up, and sit down. How tough can that be?

What would be your first step to accomplish the task? Would you rather take the time to develop a relationship with your tigers before you get in the arena? Or would you prefer to jump right in and start pushing them with all of your might toward their respective stools?

Let's say pushing did not work. How far do you think you would get by stalking them, by poking the tigers with a sharp stick and beating them with a club to get them going in the right direction? They will surely at least mildly respond if you show them who's boss.

So you start beating them, and you see one of them snarling at you, ears back. He is not happy. While you're trying to keep your eye on *that* tiger, you notice out of the corner of your eye that another one is slipping around behind you. His ears are laid back, too; his tail is twitching. Are you getting concerned yet?

Although they are solitary animals, there is a name for a grouping of tigers. A group of tigers is called a "streak".

But wait, there are three more tigers, and they're getting restless, too – and none of them is sitting on a stool. You didn't notice it at first because you were so focused on the snarling tiger and the one walking behind you, but now the other three tigers are starting to pace.

You may have initially been able to get them to move in one direction or another so they could avoid being beaten. But now *they* are stalking *you*…

How well do you think *you* would do in an arena of angry tigers? Do you think you would survive an attack from a 400 pound killer? How about *five of them*?

Maybe your tigers aren't people. Maybe they are personal habits that hold you back, and, try as you might, you find them difficult to shake. Just about the time you think you have the problem mastered, it reappears.

Maybe you don't have a streak of tigers on the prowl behind your back, but can you see the parallel here between this example and one or more aspects of your own life?

Dan Stockdale

NOTES

Taming Tigers

Releasing an eaglet into the wild. The American Eagle Foundation (www.eagles.org) is making great strides in repopulating our eagles. The American Bald Eagle has now been taken off of the endangered species list, but much work remains.

Chapter 10: Taming Tigers Secret #2 (continued)

Relationship - Part 2: The Payoffs of Building Relationship

Using 3Ts in your business and personal relationships will allow you to build better, longer-lasting relationships that are beneficial to you, your managers, your employees, and your entire organization. Granted, you probably will not single-handedly create world peace, but you *can* go a long way toward improving your world (tribe), the lives of those around you, and those who come in contact with you.

As I've said, developing relationships, whether with co-workers or critters, takes personal strength, fortitude, and a willingness to be vulnerable. You have to be able to express what your needs are in order to get someone to meet them. And in order to meet the needs of others, they must be able to communicate to you what they want. For both of you to feel free to express those needs without fear of reprisal, you must have a strong, positive relationship.

Working with animals or people, our role is to meet *their* needs, not to have them meet *ours*. Are you wondering, "But what about *me*!? Who is going to be taking care of me?"

You know what I have found? *The more I focus on meeting the needs of others, the better off – the more cared for - I am.*

"Behavior breeds behavior," remember? If you think of yourself as a leader who has a greater purpose in life than working a job (whether it is as a janitor or a CEO), you'll come to see that *all* leaders - including you - can reach their fullest potential, achieve the most success, and obtain the most resources when they begin thinking of themselves as *servant-leaders*, thriving when the focus is on creating a positive life experience for *others*.

Transference of Traits Through Relationship

Once you have established a relationship with an individual or a team, that relationship can be transferred to others. Let me give you an example. There are times when I am working on various projects that prevent me from spending the time I would like to with the animals I work with on in California. But the trainers who care for and work with the animals every day have built and maintain great relationships with the animals. As a result I can walk into an enclosure with a trainer and any tiger. As long as the trainer and I interact well, that tiger sees the relationship, and I receive transferred power by association. Positive relationship begets positive relationship.

It happens in business too when you take the time to build relationships. Transference of your good traits and the trust you have earned transfers over to other people who are associated with you. You have heard that word-of-mouth advertising is the best kind, of course. That's an example of relationship transference. When someone you trust tells you a restaurant is great or a business delivers incredible customer service, you listen, and the trust you have for that individual transfers over to the business.

Remember in the beginning of this book when we talked about anthropomorphism? Well, the expression "birds of a feather flock together" is a kind of anthropomorphic way of talking about transference. Again, those positive traits from one relationship transfer onto other relationships and individuals, which are in turn seen positively.

Trust me; you want to be in *that* flock! Management you hire, employees you supervise, or others on your team, will experience the effects of the goodwill you have worked to establish in all of your relationships.

Relationship Building can Never Stop

You can't hope to achieve your desired objectives with the people you interact with all day, every day, if you don't continually and consistently *build your relationships with them*. These relationships form the cornerstone of 3Ts. Unless the relationship is developed, nothing else will work for long. It's like building a house with a weak foundation; eventually it will crumble. Relationships hold organizations together and solidify ongoing results.

> Relationship building is an on-going process that never stops. If you're not *building* your relationships you're *destroying* them!

When working with a primate, a trainer doesn't quit paying attention to him, stroking him and working to establish a bond, just because the primate has learned a behavior. Or when I walk by a tiger's enclosure, I don't ignore the animal because I got the behavior I wanted out of her at yesterday's event. It must be ongoing and consistent. *The relationship-building must never stop.*

At home, we don't stop trying to build our relationship with our spouse after we get a ring and an "I do." If we did, our relationship wouldn't last long, would it? Or, even if it survived, it would most likely be a superficial connection at best. *The relationship-building must never stop.*

And most of us patiently teach our children new skills. We know we can't force them to walk before they are ready. And we don't stop helping them learn to talk once they have that walking thing down. Similarly, when our children don't speak in fluent and complete sentences from the get-go, we don't say, "What's the use? He's never going to learn to say anything but 'Mama' and 'Dada.' I give up." Our work as trainers must be on-going and consistent. *The relationship-building must never stop.*

Clearly, most of us are patient and unwavering in building relationships within our families over a lifetime. But it fails to occur to many of us that the same must be true for relationships *outside* of our family unit, especially in business, if we hope to succeed as leaders over the long haul.

The Importance of Trust in Developing Relationships

Even the most driven among us can be inherently lazy when it comes to relationships. When our personal or professional lives are going well, we tend to take our relationships for granted. We stop building and working on them when we're getting the behaviors we want from others. Until someone does something we don't want them to do... then we often jump immediately to negative reinforcement in order to quickly "correct" that behavior.

In tiger training, establishing and maintaining a positive relationship with the animal leads to developing trust when the trainer is in the tiger's enclosure. In the "seemingly insane" department, one of the trainers I have worked with can sometimes be caught off-stage in the tiger enclosure, catching a quick catnap with a cat he raised. She is a 400-pound Bengal tiger. Crazy as it may seem to catnap with such a huge cat, the two of them have a relationship based on total trust, so behavior that may seem strange to us is no different for the trainer and his tiger than falling asleep in your own home with your family dog at the foot of the bed might be for you.

The opposite of trust, for both animals and humans, is fear. When trust has never been developed or has been betrayed, animals react with fear, whether it is a cowering abused dog or a defensive, attacking tiger.

Can you remember a situation in your life where you reacted with fear to a betrayal of your trust?

Trainers know that animals trust us to train in an ethical manner, and to attend to their needs, like a clean enclosure, food, and water. When we have built a relationship, they trust that we will not come into their space and give them anything negative, even when they don't deliver the behavior we want. They learn that the worst thing that will happen in training is a neutral response from their trainers. We will simply stand there, not acknowledging anything for a moment, then move on.

When we work with exotic animals in their environment and have built a relationship with them, they have no reason to distrust us.

With people, you build trust not only by giving attention and meeting needs, but also by not being *un*trustworthy, by not acting irrational and punishing those who don't behave exactly as you'd like them to.

Maybe you have heard the expression "It's better to be feared than disobeyed." Maybe that is even your operating principle in your life or work. But whether you are working with real tigers, or 'tigers' in your workplace, the fact it that it's better to take the route that will build *trust* (the opposite of fear) and *relationship*.

Obviously, humans have a far greater ability to understand the consequences of their behaviors than tigers do. They also understand more complex rules and boundaries than a real tiger can and can choose to be manipulative, so there are certain "bad" behaviors you can't ignore in the way you would with animals.

You can't just stand by and ignore it when an employee treats a customer rudely, for example, and then tells you the customer deserved it. You must address the situation, and likely even punish the behavior. When an employee's negative action has the potential to have a harmful impact on the business's finances, employee morale, or customer service, you must address the situation. The severity of how it is addressed depends on the seriousness of the employee's action. Sometimes we have to address employee issues in a manner that we never would consider when actually training an animal.

So, how does the idea of punishment work within the concept of "Taming Tigers"? Well, it depends upon the attitude of the person with whom you are working. Sometimes our "tigers" are unpredictable. Your tiger may become angry and vengeful or, they may see the validity of your concern and immediately change their behavior. Frankly, in this scenario, the important issue is that you address the problem. Their response is not your foremost concern.

Q&A: A Question of Trust? Here are the Answers!
What if you are a CEO who needs to develop a relationship with your "tiger" in order to see the organization progress, and that tiger is someone who is considerably lower than you on the organization's "food chain"? If that person is a different "breed," what are some of the things you need to know to establish strong relationships?

How can you build trust and a relationship with those whose position in relation to you may make them somewhat uncomfortable or possibly even make them inherently distrust *you*?

And *should* you trust a person who you know would really love to have your job?

The key to building trust lies in open, honest, effective communication. If you are the CFO and the divisional vice presidents catch you in a lie, how much trust will be there?

I worked with a company in the mid-1990's that epitomized distrust. I knew I was working with the wrong group of individuals when we were having a meeting at the company headquarters. It was a rainy afternoon, and all five regional VP's were near the end of a long day filled with operational challenges.

Toward the middle of the afternoon, the comptroller came into the room, and we expressed our frustration over the company's lack of timeliness paying the bills for our operating units. The sad truth was that frequently the electric company was going to the properties to shut off the electric due to non-payment. In addition, the office staff actually began to become accustomed to having the phones cut off. And vendors were never paid unless they filed a lawsuit against the company. Needless to say, these scenarios, playing out month after month, were frustrating, and a deep sense of distrust of the corporate office developed throughout all levels of the organization.

The last straw, however, was at the end of the meeting. We had had just spent the entire day forcefully expressing our frustration over the lack of financial integrity at the corporate office. Then, the comptroller sternly confided that he had wiped out over $5 million in accounts payable from the books, thus allowing the company to reach its quarterly projections for the investors.

Trust? If there was *any* left after months of utility disconnections and endless vendor threats, I can assure you that the well of trust went completely dry as he left the room. Not only had they been misappropriating money from the company coffers that should have been used to pay vendors, now they were falsifying legal documents and altering financial records to make the numbers reflect a false 'reality' to investors. Trust them? Never. Integrity? Not an ounce. That was a negative relationship, through and through.

So, how do you build trust? As I've already mentioned, through open, honest communication and actions that you back up with integrity. This is vital at all levels of the organization, but especially at the top.

> How do we build trust? Through open, honest communication.

To be sure, for all of the negative examples of creating a lack of trust in corporate America, there are numerous positive ones as well.

One automotive organization I am familiar with routinely undercuts the competition when they're asked to give a bid on work. But upon further examination of their financial records, I found that they habitually came in with a final price even lower than the already low bid initially quoted.

When I asked the owner about the discrepancy that greatly favored the consumer, he emphasized that the automotive repair service industry has a bad reputation for taking advantage of its customers. He has made it his policy for years to single-handedly attempt to dispel that negative notion that has been planted in the minds of consumers by decades of unscrupulous service centers. Trust them for future repairs? You bet! Integrity? They live it and breathe it every day! They build relationships that are entirely positive, through and through.

Building Relationships Builds Results
Does your work rely on receiving timely reports from others, such as financials? If receiving monthly financial statements within the first ten days of the month is one of your tigers, read on. Just because the accounting department produces the financial reports for June's operations by July 10th, you should not assume that you always will. Your continued support, reinforcement, and appreciation of accounting's performance determines if you will continue to achieve your objectives – such as receiving timely reports. That is building a relationship. *That is training.*

Now you might be tempted to say, "Accounting is being *paid* to produce the reports. It's their *job*! If they don't do it, I will find someone who *will*!" That is not building a relationship. *That is taming.*

As their boss, do you have a right to make this statement or to have this attitude, even if you don't speak it? Of course you do.

Is that attitude the *best* method, however, to achieve ongoing positive results? Probably not.

Developing a relationship by training with positive reinforcement techniques will be the *best* way. Regardless of the task, you can achieve your desired results by utilizing the talents of others in such a way that the individuals involved feel rewarded and affirmed for their accomplishments.

Positive Reinforcement and Bonding to Build Relationships
You don't have to be an extroverted, "touchy-feely" type to know this is true: Work is not a sterile, emotion-free environment. There are all kinds of relationships there, like it or not, so you might as well learn to utilize them to the advantage of the organization.

Bonding is essential for successful positive reinforcement with animals *and* with humans. If my neighbor, the abusive pet owner, had gotten to know his dog, communicated with and bonded with him, he would have been far less likely to want to intimidate and hurt the dog. In the same way, once you have bonded even a little bit with your child or your spouse - or developed a relationship with your employee, a client, or a prospect - your natural tendency will be to interact with them in a mutually beneficial manner.

Now, you may be thinking, "Maybe you are right about the people in my life outside of work – I could definitely work on bonding better in *those* relationships – but I have no intention of 'bonding' with my staff. They are my *staff*, for goodness sake, not my friends and family!"

To be clear, I am not necessarily talking about having all those who work for and with you over to your house for dinner, visiting their place to play cards, or, while you are at it, going on vacation together.

The truth of the matter, however, is that in our ever-changing workplace, the role of the supervisor in many organizations has evolved into a more informal one – quasi-friend, sounding board, even psychotherapist. The personal - work boundaries our parents experienced have been greatly blurred.

> The role of supervisor has evolved into a more informal one – quasi-friend, sounding board, parent, even psychotherapist! Welcome to Generation Y!

Although you may not want to be roommates, it's healthy to develop a spirit of camaraderie with those you work with so they know you're truly concerned about them and their success. By doing so, you'll develop a cohesive team that cares about the success of the group as well as the accomplishments of their peers.

Dan Stockdale

Concern Creates Camaraderie

How do you create a spirit of camaraderie? It is actually fairly simple. All you have to do is *be genuinely concerned.* Here are some examples: A co-worker mentions in passing that her son is playing in the baseball tournament. Or maybe, a subordinate says that his child is going off to college.

Usually, this kind of information goes in one ear and out the other. It's not business-related data, and we don't file it away in our minds. There's way too much "more important" stuff that we have to focus on, right?

You create relationships – you bond – by being *genuinely concerned* about those in your tribe and what is happening in their lives. Make an effort: ask how the baseball game went, how the child is adjusting to college life, or how the parents are adjusting to life without the child at home.

I promise you will be amazed at how good you feel by making others feel good with just a little bit of attention and concern. And when you start showing concern for others, you create camaraderie, and that can be contagious. I also guarantee that you'll find that connecting is a lot simpler than you'd imagined.

For some people, in a perfect world everyone would check their emotions and the personal part of themselves at the office door. They would not carry that "baggage" into the workplace, and would totally focus on work issues while at work, and then pick their personal lives back up on their way home.

But it doesn't happen that way, does it? I remember when I was growing up, as soon as I would get home from school, I would call my dad at work to let him know I was home. I still recall the phone number. We never stayed on the phone long, but it was, nonetheless, a personal interruption in his business day. An interruption that his boss could have taken issue with, but didn't.

Chemistry Matters

Before we go any further in our discussion of relationship, let's take a quick look at the role chemistry plays. Different animals learn at different rates. One tiger may learn a behavior in two or three days, while another tiger can take two or three months to learn the same behavior.

Learning speed can also depend on trainer effectiveness. One trainer may be able to work well with a particular animal but is not able to work as well with another one.

There is definitely chemistry – good and bad – between trainers and animals, just as between humans. Like everyone, I am sure you have experienced being able to get along better with some people than you do with others. There is a clear lesson here about our relationships: Many of us will beat ourselves up when a job doesn't work out, or a relationship with a boss or a friend or a family member isn't going as we'd like it to, but it *can* just be bad chemistry.

An essential aspect of the 3Ts is learning to understand that we should not take what is essentially a matter of chemistry and make it a personal attack.

When a particular employee has a great skill set, but is not working out well in your department, maybe the answer is not to terminate the employee. Maybe arranging for a transfer into another area is most appropriate.

"Bad" chemistry isn't usually anybody's fault; it's just not the right fit. Don't try to force the fit, and be sure to allow the employee to exit gracefully.

Dan Stockdale

NOTES

Taming Tigers

Dan Stockdale

Chapter 10: Taming Tigers Secret #2 (continued)

Relationship - Part 3: Building Business Relationships

I'll give you three examples of how you can use the Taming Tigers Techniques to build relationships and help tame your tigers in business.

Let's look at an example of building relationships using 3Ts at work in a business that typically uses the negative model: an auto dealership, where big numbers and high production are oftentimes more important than retaining the sales force.

Even if you are not involved in auto sales at all, you probably know that the turnover rate among salespeople is remarkably high. Ever tried to find the person who sold you a car a couple of years before when you start shopping around for another one? That's a pretty rare find.

The pressure to make sales and meet quotas can be too much even for dedicated professionals. Many sales managers, whose livelihood is also dependent on those sales, believe they have no choice but to practice negative techniques, covertly or overtly, even at the risk of extremely high turnover among their people. They can only envision the short-term, and believe that if they lose their best while cleaning house of the rest, there are plenty of others out there who will take the job, and probably work harder, too.

This negative, short-term attitude about the sales force can't help but translate into a negative, short-term view of the customer. So one negative relationship dynamic begets another. See how that works?

Dan Stockdale

A leader who's ready to build relationships with 3Ts will begin by taking the focus off short-term results and immediate gratification, emphasizing instead a long-term commitment. If auto dealers develop long-term relationships with customers, they can not only sell them a car today, but three years from now, and then again when the customer's children start driving, and when the spouse wants to upgrade, and so forth. Instead of just making a single sale today, car dealerships focused on long-term success seek repeat sales that will come down the road, so to speak.

Feasibly, a positive sales leader can keep a customer or client forever when focused on the long-term, and while some costs may go up, those loyal customers will bring more customers with them, all the while increasing revenue and profit. Indeed, car dealers can develop long-term, more productive relationships with customers by first developing the same sort of relationships with their sales staffs.

This example holds true in all of your relationships, at home, at work, and in the community. *Long-term, cooperative focus yields long-term positive results in every aspect of our lives, even if there are some short-term sacrifices.*

Banking on Relationships! - The Short and Long-Term Payoffs of Relationships
We can look at investing in relationship another way, with an analogy that puts the difference in simple black and white terms using the dynamics of money. For you concrete, sequential, analytical types – like me – we can quantify this example in simple numbers.

If you eke out a dollar a day in profit by using an effective, short-term method, at the end of the year you will have generated $365, right? However, if you take a different approach and are willing to start with the smaller reward of just one penny in profit the first day of the year but increase your profit by an extra penny a day every day, do you think this approach might pay off?

If you believe you are relationship impaired and only looking for the instant payoff, you are better off not risking it. Just earn your dollar a day by finding a new customer every time you need to make a sale. Trying a new approach will not earn you nearly as much money the first month…or the second month…or the third month.

But, if you are willing to develop relationships with long-term, repetitive results, at the end of one year, you will find that you have earned almost twice as much money as you would if you'd chosen to keep earning a buck a day.

Check out this table:

	$1 a day	1¢ plus 1¢ each day
January	31.00	4.65
February	28.00	13.95
March	31.00	23.25
April	30.00	32.55
May	31.00	41.85
June	30.00	51.15
July	31.00	60.45
August	31.00	69.75
September	30.00	79.05
October	31.00	88.35
November	30.00	97.65
December	31.00	106.95
TOTALS	365.00	669.60

Okay, I know the numbers are not earth shattering! But what about Year Two, and Year Three, and Year Ten? How would those numbers look?

The payoff was not very good for the short term. It took time, several months, for you to begin realizing better gains. But if you want to experience long-term success, the choice is easy. It's worth it to take a few short-term hits for the long-term good.

Relationships Save Time (and Money) in the Long Term
Here's a third example. Let's say you're a motivational speaker who has a presentation called "Managing Miscellaneous Monkeys." You can work your tail off trying to find a new group to speak to every week. Or you can offer additional services, ask for referrals, give discounts for multi-year contracts, offer ongoing coaching services, write articles for your client's internal publications, or offer many other valuable and creative services.

You can focus on the short term and speak once or develop long-term relationships that will build your business for years to come. Not to mention the far greater positive impact you'll make on your clients and their organizations by being involved with them for months or years instead of just hours.

Creating appropriate, genuine connections with customers and employees is POWERFUL. You can harness that power to achieve wealth for both your organization and for yourself.

Build Relationships with Sincerity: Proactive Availability
Essential to developing relationships, "proactive availability" is a concept of creating a culture within your department, division, or company in which you're intentionally visible and accessible. It goes beyond a simple "open door" policy. When you're proactively available, you purposely reach out to those within your organization, both internally and externally, who you have the most ability to help so you can create a positive impact on others.

I once worked for a corporation (we'll call it ABC Corp.) that was one of several that wanted to buy and manage an office complex in California. The complex was owned by a non-profit, community organization. When the seller decided to put the buildings on the market, our company submitted an offer. We knew we would need the support of the building's tenants to ensure that our offer would win out over others'.

> Proactive availability – It goes beyond an "open door" policy. Roll up your sleeves and start talking to your "tigers".

So ABC's president did the unexpected. She rolled up her sleeves and started talking to everyone she could, including the building's cleaning crew. She went to every office in the building, asking what issues and challenges tenants faced and what she could do to help.

She was very sincere in her desire to help the tenants. However, she also had to be careful not to let others perceive her as a lobbyist. She exercised caution so that she didn't ever cross over into the managers' business. She just proactively made herself available, searching out the needs and how she could best meet them, *building relationships*.

As a result of her efforts, tenants started writing letters to the editor of the newspaper, showing up at meetings, and making phone calls on her behalf, all without being asked.

She developed relationships by being proactively available to everyone and showing a sincere interest in them. And sincerity is a key point. If they had an issue, she did not just smile and nod and say, "We will take care of that." She really *did* something about it.

Emerging from the Corporate Cocoon
When an executive comes out of the corporate cocoon and begins to make herself available, a glorious outcome often emerges: Relationships flourish and differences tend to disappear.

Put old ideas about hierarchy behind you to make proactive availability work for you. When you come out of your cocoon, so to speak, you go as far down the organizational structure as necessary to make contact. When you talk to the folks several levels removed from you, finding out what is important to them, and working to meet those needs, you establish deep-rooted relationships.

Dan Stockdale

It can be as simple as saying "Hi!" as you walk down the hallway.
Most people, sadly, have come to not expect that, and simple
pleasantries can make a huge difference in employees' loyalty and
willingness to work hard for you and for the organization.

When they see a suit walking down the hallway, they expect to be
ignored, so they react positively when you speak to them and ask,
"Hey, how's your son doing? I heard about that fifty-yard play in the
game last weekend. That's great!"

Very early in my career, I was visiting with the president of a hospital
group in Ohio. We had spent a considerable amount of time in his
very elaborate, meticulously designed office. As we finished our
meeting, we walked together out of his suite and down the hall toward
one of the main corridors of the hospital. I was shocked when, as we
emerged from his office, his gaze fell to the floor and stayed there,
rarely looking up as we passed nurses, doctors, patients, and families.
This corporate leader's personality wilted at the mere sight of those
who looked to him for leadership.

> **Come out of the cocoon! Earn accolades!**

Yes, he was a reasonably successful person
and was very confident within the protection
of his office cocoon. But when he emerged
into the rest of his world, he made no effort
to connect with anyone. His walk through
the hospital could have yielded him scores
of accolades with those he led. Instead, he received uneasy, fleeting
looks from those who desired to connect with him. Either he did not
want to be bothered by them, or he simply did not know how to
communicate. Either way, it was not good.

Like animals, people are *very* perceptive. Animals immediately
perceive a threat, and they also perceive when people have their best
interests at heart. *Both animals and people will rise – or descend – to
meet your expectations.* When animals or people feel that they share a
cooperative relationship with you, they will work hard, knowing that
you care for them.

Our hospital executive? He stayed on as long as he could: fighting turnover, losing employees to competing healthcare organizations, and trying to keep things copasetic with the Board. Eventually though, the hospital was forced to restructure.

The corporate cocoon exists in many organizations, and many executives use it as a place of refuge, choosing a simple 'chain-of-command' communication model. Emerging from the cocoon takes a more complex style of management, but it will allow you to improve your relationships and improve your organization. Emerge!

Dan Stockdale

TIGER TALKING POINTS

1. How do you create a spirit of camaraderie?

2. What is one of the best ways to get the individuals on a team to work well together?

3. Should leaders be focused on short-term results or long-term commitment? Why?

Taming Tigers

Dan Stockdale

Chapter 10: Taming Tigers Secret #2 (continued)

Relationships - Part 4: Striking a Balance

The Best Relationships Balance Positive and Negative

Humans and animals, as I mentioned earlier, are different in many respects, and training them is different in that with tigers, or any animal for that matter, you never use a negative or punishment to achieve a behavior. With humans, sometimes, you can, and must.

With people, there is a time and a place for punishment or negative reinforcement, when you have to deal with situations by implementing unpleasant consequences, but you must *balance* that with positive support .

Maybe Suzy has a problem arriving late to work, and let's assume the employee handbook says "5 episodes of being tardy within a 90 day period will result in a verbal warning." As her supervisor, you have an obligation to issue a verbal warning, which is a punishment.

But, just because Suzy is tardy, does that mean you ignore the fact that she has the highest sales in the company? Absolutely not. You don't keep the focus on the negative but redirect it to the positive. What is done is done, and you then move right back into positive mode.

But, maybe she is *not* a star sales performer. Maybe she is also struggling to meet her sales goals. Well, now is your chance: Write her up. Hey, as a matter of fact if she has prior documented offenses in her file, go ahead and fire her! We might as well kick her while she is down, right?

Dan Stockdale

Wrong! If we look at our relationship with her as a long-term one, we will strive to treat her the same way we'd treat any other employee – including the Salesperson of the Month.

When it comes to taming your own "tigers," you will find that the more you use 3Ts, the less often you will be called upon to use the punishment or negative model. Balance, in other words, eventually tips toward the positive side of the scale almost exclusively.

For long-term positive benefit, 3Ts always works better than negative methods because when you develop positive relationships, people feel and see your appreciation and will reward *your* loyalty and respect with *their* loyalty and respect. That's a great relationship right there!

It's Positive to "Just Say 'No'"
Creating positive relationships doesn't mean you never say "No." It includes discipline as well as reward. In animal training, saying "No" is known as an "aversive stimulus." It may seem negative, because it's not based on reward, but an effective aversive stimulus is never detrimental and never hurts the animal.

Think of it this way: It is never "positive" to get hurt, so it is always better for an animal– or a child - to hear the word "No" than for him or her to, for example, ingest a chemical.

Kids. No, Not Goats. Children!
If you have raised children, you know that any punishment or negative reinforcement you must use when training them is far more effective if the child trusts you. If children perceive you to be an uncaring, uncompassionate parent with an unpleasant temper, and there is no established trusting relationship, then your attempts at discipline, while effective in the short-term, will be less effective and will have a negative effect on your relationship in the long-term. Children will not believe you are implementing negative reinforcement out of love or concern but only because you are mean.

If they don't trust you, how can they believe that you know what is best for them? You have not established a relationship wherein they have the expectation that you are ultimately looking out for their best interests. What's more, without trust, they have no motivation to respond as you want them to.

On the other hand, when kids feel loved and trusted, and you set a curfew, for example, they are less likely to assume the curfew was decided upon arbitrarily or punitively and will trust instead that there must be some legitimate reason for it. They are less likely to push boundaries if trust has been fostered between you.

Children who have a strong relationship with their parents, who believe they are loved, and who have learned that their parents have their best interests at heart, will exhibit fewer behaviors that *require* negative responses from their parents.

This is also true of tigers and other animals, and it is definitely true of everyone you relate to in the professional world. We rarely learn in our corporate jungle to engender trust among those with whom we work. They learn, instead, to "trust no one," and to look out for Number One at all costs.

Those who have had positive relationships in their personal lives always seem to have gained them through divine intervention and the grace of God. Far too many people, however, have had few if any, positive, trusting relationships. So they have no model for that behavior, making it exceedingly difficult to exercise it at home and at work. If you grew up and spent your entire adulthood continuously in negative situations, without learning to trust, you can't help but be untrusting. But, there is good news! Over time, by learning and practicing 3Ts, you can shed that baggage and learn an entirely new approach. It's never too late!

Similarly, it is not *detrimental* to my son when I ground him from his car, computer, or video games for not doing homework. Granted, *he* thinks it's the end of the world, but most parents would agree that it's for his long-term good.

Dan Stockdale

Using Negative Techniques to Create a Positive Result
One good thing about working with humans versus exotic animals is that humans have the ability to reason and understand more than animals do. So when you train people using 3Ts, you can use techniques that should never be used with animals. This more diverse collection of techniques – some positive, some slightly aversive, and when necessary, some negative – gives you the opportunity to achieve a positive/negative balance.

For example, as a consultant, if I am called into an organization with severe financial issues to help get them back on track, I can assure you that some of the folks there aren't going to like me. I'm being paid to look at *all* expenditures, put controls in place, and look at *every* position to see which, if any, can be eliminated or reassigned.

Then I'm going to move immediately to the revenue side of the equation to see what revenue possibilities are being overlooked. What services or products are not being effectively marketed? How can offerings be expanded? What needs do existing clients have that are not being met? Why do customers not buy the product or service? And on and on.

You may be thinking I sound hypocritical. Here I am purporting to advocate a 'kinder, gentler' workplace, while I am also saying that I will go into a failing organization with an attitude of "Heads are gonna roll!" What gives?

Balance. This includes the ability to adjust management style, moment by moment, based upon the needs of the situation and organization. At times, a perceived negative change in one individual's position actually can have an overall positive effect for those employees remaining and for the organization as a whole.

So when I'm consulting, I may adopt one management style with the VP of Marketing who is doing a stellar job, yet moments later, I may take a much more aggressive posture with the VP of Regulatory Compliance. I adjust my management style to the situation.

> **Achieve balance for optimal Tiger Taming success!**

Sounds simple, doesn't it? But how often do you see leaders who respond to *every* situation the same way? Or leaders who haven't been trained to alter their management style as needed? Or leaders who operate on feelings and emotions instead of facts and logic?

Seek to achieve *balance*. In general, adopt a positive approach but don't hesitate to take a more aggressive posture in business when that's what is called for. This is, after all, business. The very survival of the organization and the livelihood of the employees could depend upon your ability to perceive what is needed at that point in time in order to tame your organization's tigers.

TIGER TALKING POINTS

1. Why do we sometimes achieve good results with the negative model of interaction?

2. Does the negative model ever yield any undesirable results? If so, what are they?

3. Do managers have any ethical obligations? If so, to who?

4. How would you get a streak of tigers on their pedestals?

5. How does a human's ability to reason and understand affect the methods we use to achieve change?

6. What is balance?

Taming Tigers

Dan Stockdale

Chapter 10: Taming Tigers Secret #2 (continued)

Relationship - Part 5: Altruism Bestows Power

Webster's Dictionary defines altruism as "Regard for others, both natural and moral; devotion to the interests of others; brotherly kindness; opposed to egoism or selfishness."

Conventional wisdom states that there is not much of a place for such a concept in business; it is a weakness. But this is a fallacy. Practicing altruism is actually a *strong* behavior that builds relationships. Strength in business *does not* mean being *inflexible* but in being adaptable in the business environment of fast-paced progress that we all operate within.

Wild Altruism
Altruism and compassion may seem like odd terms to use in a discussion about wild animals... and a discussion of business relationships, for that matter! But animals in the wild actually exhibit altruism as a means of species survival, putting the needs of the group ahead of their own personal needs, even of their own lives.

> Altruism – Regard for others, both natural and moral; devotion to the interests of others; brotherly kindness; opposed to egoism or selfishness.

With animals, altruism is exhibited when behaviors are shown that may be a disadvantage to the individual animal but that may benefit the entire group. For example, when an animal calls out a warning to other animals at the sign of a predator, they risk revealing their own location to the killer. Such instinctive cooperative behavior may ultimately be detrimental to the individual animal, but it nonetheless contributes to the survival of the group. It really gives new meaning to "taking one for the team", doesn't it?

Tiger-Trainer Altruism
In the tiger-trainer relationship, you will frequently see trainers putting the needs of their animals above their own personal needs. As I mentioned earlier, it is not unusual for trainers to work day in and day out for no pay, just to ensure that the animals are well cared for. Too, trainers must be compassionate in every daily interaction with animals, treating them with understanding and being sensitive to their needs.

Like house cats, tigers will sleep or rest between 14 and 18 hours a day. Therefore, they are generally quite content with spending most of their time hanging out in their enclosures napping. By the same token, they are generally taken for several hours to a daily romp around an exercise arena. The tigers enjoy that time, and so the altruistic attitude is for the trainer to meet that need. Just like all of us, trainers get busy, too, but they don't skip the tigers' play time just because they are too busy with chores.

In other words, tigers' needs don't change just because the trainers' needs do. And compassionate trainers understand and nurture that, consistently. In the same way, if you have a tiger who is a picky eater, you don't starve or punish it to try to change its eating habits. You have compassion for its different dietary needs and work to accommodate them.

Practicing Altruism with your "Tigers"
What about the tigers who work with and for you? Do you spend time daily trying to help, understand and nurture them? Seriously, do you? Or, do you spend your time trying to change them? When was the last time you sat down with an often overlooked employee, one on one, to find out about them and their needs?

If altruism works to train animals that have the potential to kill in a split second, can you imagine that it might work to train the humans on your team? When people are your "tigers," you may not have to worry about them killing you, but they *can* attack and be dangerous in other ways.

Fail to be altruistic with your clients and you will soon find them gone. Fail to be altruistic whenever possible with your internal customers - your employees - and they too will be gone – along with the experience, connections, and relationships they developed while working for you. Altruism truly plays a pivotal role in the development of relationships.

You must be compassionate and sensitive to others' needs in the workplace. For example, many employees now have to cope with aging parents in addition to all of the other responsibilities of life. Being as flexible as you can to accommodate the needs of those who must care for an elderly or ailing parent goes a long way toward establishing the employee-employer relationship.

Many offices have rather arbitrary opening and closing times, and *everyone* must be in by 8am and out by 5pm, no matter whether their jobs involve them answering the phones or greeting visitors who walk through the door. If it does not really matter whether someone works eight hours starting at noon or 4 AM or in two four-hour shifts, and people need to do so to accommodate the needs of their families, can you exercise altruism and flexibility to find a way to make that work?

Of course the needs of the business come first, but doesn't it make sense to do whatever you possibly can to strengthen the relationships and loyalty of your staff whenever possible?

I am not advocating total organizational anarchy here – and you will, in fact, find that most people *want* to work 8–5, have done so forever, and make it work quite nicely, thank you very much – but I am suggesting that flexibility and adaptability on your part will go a long way to ensure the loyalty and hard work of your employees with specific needs, and it can be a lot more do-able than you initially believed.

Will you be criticized from those within your organization who are rigid in their observance of rules? Quite possibly you will. You have to be ready to explain, however, that this is not a matter of preferential treatment or soft management; it is a matter of creating a culture where individual needs matter.

Training in Altruism: 'Ask!'

In fundraising, there's an old saying that goes, "You're never going to get what you're after unless you make the ask." In other words, no matter how wonderful your cause is, almost no one says, "That sounds great. Here's a big pile of money," unless you *ask* for it. You have to tell the donor what you need, and ask them to meet that need, before they will give you what you want.

Once you have mastered the practice of altruism to build relationships, you can you direct others to develop these same skills, training them to be aware of others' needs are, and giving them the leeway to meet those needs whenever possible.

First, train by example. Altruism is going to be a hard sell if they don't see you practicing it yourself.

Show others the power of a simple *ask*. Train a sales manager, for example, to *ask* sales staff what their customers need and how management can make it easier for them to provide for their customers' needs. Train a VP of Operations, to *ask* district managers and site managers what he or she can do to help them. You get the picture.

Of course, you can also conduct formal training in altruism and relationship building, or hire a qualified consultant to train, so that your staff knows *how* to ask the questions, *what* questions to ask, *when* to ask them, and how to respond. But the most effective way to teach is by example.

NOTES

Dan Stockdale

Chapter 10: Taming Tigers Secret #2 (continued)

Relationship - Part 6: Learning and the Million $ Question

Don't Wait Until it's Too Late

Every day, people give business over to a vendor's competition, not because of a cheaper price, but because the competing vendor met all of their needs and their current vendor did not. The competition simply took better care of the organization than the original vendor; they built a strong relationship by paying more attention.

Recently, I cancelled a contract with a vendor because, for the three years I worked with the company, no one ever communicated with me: to check on the quality of service being provided or even to introduce themselves. They were getting the money every month for the equipment we rented, and that was all that mattered. And, frankly, it was very easy to cancel that contract, since I had never seen or heard from anyone at the company except when I had to make calls for tech support. If I had had a face to put with the service, some kind – any kind – of relationship, cancelling would have been *much* more difficult.

> If you are in sales, and *everyone* is, meet the needs of your customers and make sure they know their business is appreciated.

Once we sent a cancellation notice, the company's president seemed to suddenly decide to start calling his customers, wanting to know why I went to the competition. I knew I was not the only one, and I told him the truth: He had operated blissfully in a vacuum for many years. Somebody else saw that market and decided they wanted a piece of it, so they came in, started marketing with attentive service, establishing *relationships* with their clients instead of merely providing service, and the original vendor lost half his business. Nobody knew who he was, except someone that they sent a check to every month, so they had no qualms about going with a vendor who better met their needs.

If you are in sales, be sure your customers feel appreciated and their needs are met to the best of your ability. Build *relationships* with them and *never* take them for granted. If you do, I can assure you someone will begin showing your customers the attention they deserve.

Oh yes, and now is probably a good time to mention that we are *all* in sales. "But I'm the Senior VP of Operations!" you may retort. Or you might reply "I'm just a paramedic. I have no customers!" I understand how you feel and I vehemently fought the notion of being in sales for years. But I slowly learned that *everyone* is in sales.

If you are the Senior VP of Operations and you haven't effectively sold your skills, ability and worth to the CEO and Board, how long do you believe you will be employed? You might say, "My results speak for themselves." And you may be correct. Your *results* are your deliverables. Just as an accountants deliverable may be a tax return.

Your employment is a sales transaction. You are selling your time and talents and someone or some organization has agreed that they would like to buy them. Regardless of position or employer, it is a pure sales transaction.

So, if your boss is actually your *customer*, how happy is this customer with your customer service?

Learning Others' Needs: You Must Communicate!
That company president did the right thing by calling me and the other clients he lost, though who knows if he would use what we told him to improve service in the future.

If one (or, heaven forbid, *more* than one) of your clients leaves, you need to follow up and find out which of their needs weren't met. If you have worked to establish a relationship with them in the past, you may be able to win them back.

If, for example, you ask what that former client needed that they didn't find in your organization, and you discover that your competitor made a small variation in a product or contract terms that better suited them, you could go back and make that revision to your own product or contract, and thereby meet that need.

And here's a neat trick: Substitute "your valuable employees" for "clients" and "their new employer" for "competitor" in that example, and you have found the keys to identifying and meeting the needs of your internal customers – your employees – as well.

Over the years, I have consulted for dozens of organizations and have started my fair share of businesses as well, and I know this is absolutely true: Simply *ask* your clients and customers what their needs are, and they will tell you.

What's more, if you promptly follow up with them on their concerns and desires, you get extra points for being pro-active. Then, when you solve the problem for them, you become a superstar!

You don't need a Harvard MBA or superior analytical skills. All you need to do is say, "Tell me three things I can do to make things better for you." Though it sounds simple, it's rarely done in a personal, sincere manner, followed by immediate action and feedback.

> The million dollar question: *"Tell me three things I can do to make things better for you"?*

As technology has evolved, we often attempt to gather any needed feedback via electronic methods; however, in many circumstances nothing can replace the personal touch. When a real person looks you in the eye and sincerely asks what you need to make your life better – and then follows through with what you have stated – you are on your way to establishing an unshakeable, valuable relationship.

Think about it, how effective would a trainer be if he sat in the office and sent an email to the tigers to see how they were doing? Absurd? Yes! But the point is simple. You can't have a real relationship unless you are present.

Meeting Needs, Once You've Discovered Them
The only way you can improve a relationship is by meeting another's needs, and the only way you can learn about those needs is through relationship! Though this may seem paradoxical, it's not difficult to do.

Only managers who actively work at establishing and maintaining relationships with employees can effectively communicate with them and learn workers' needs and meet them.

So, take a moment and consider these questions:

- What are some needs your employees might have that you may have overlooked in the past? Don't know? Ask!

- How can you identify those needs and meet them?

- What can you do to make your employees feel respected and appreciated?

- What can you do to let your boss know that you are in his or her corner?

- What needs does your spouse or significant other have? What can you do to meet those needs?

- What about the kids? Sure, you provide a roof over their heads, but what else do they need from you? Time? Respect? Love?

The good news is that it can be remarkably easy to build relationships by meeting needs when you are paying attention and are ready, willing, and able to do what it takes.

> It can be remarkably easy to build relationships by meeting needs when you are paying attention and are ready, willing and able to do what it takes.

Here is an example from the animal world of meeting needs to develop relationships: Kara is a tiger I've worked with on the West Coast. When trainers take Kara out into the canyon to work with her, she lies down and eats grass for about 10 minutes until she vomits the grass back up to cleanse her digestive system. After that, she is ready to work. Though other tigers can come out of their enclosure ready to go to work, Kara's routine is different. She knows what she needs and has shown the trainers what those needs are; they respect those needs, are willing to meet them, and don't try to make her start working until she has gone through her little ritual.

Building relationships with humans by meeting needs often can be just as simple. For example, some employees probably don't care much about the brand of pen or paperclip they use, but how about letting staff order the supplies they would like, rather than what has *always* been ordered? If letting the creative types order neon sticky pads instead of pastels will increase their productivity even a little bit by making them happier, ultimately, the bottom line improves with this little morale boost. So isn't it worth investing a couple of extra cents?

While some needs are a lot more complex than this, by beginning with "baby steps," you'll see how effectively meeting even small needs helps to build relationships.

Improve the Quality of "Real" Lives

Hopefully, your staff does not feel the need to regurgitate before the start of each work day, but what *do* they need to do their best work? In my years of experience, the most common employee needs relate to their quality of life.

Establishing a strong relationship can begin by simply realizing that, like you, everyone has a life outside of the office walls. You must be willing to let them have that life if you want to have a good, strong relationship with them. In turn, your willingness becomes a *powerful* positive reinforcer, enabling you to establish the behaviors you want.

Flexibility with work hours remains a major priority for many people, and is a fantastic reinforcer when you can bend enough to meet the needs of employees whose work hours won't negatively affect the organization.

For example, you might allow a parent to work from 6:30 AM until 2:30 PM so that he or she can be there when the children get off the school bus. Or, even if your company policy is only two weeks' vacation a year, you can let someone take an extra two weeks off without pay in order to go visit a sick parent or to get reacquainted with a spouse who is returning from a stint overseas.

The Power of Positive Relationships

What can you expect when you establish positive relationships and help others to do so as well? First, when you put others' needs before your own, for the good of the organization, you can expect *your* relationships to improve. Put others before yourself and you will find them doing the same for you, showing concern for your needs and seeking to fulfill them as much as possible.

Does that seem way too touchy, feely for you? Think of it this way: do you belong to a city club or a country club? Or, do you ever entertain your clients at a nice restaurant? Or, do you ever stay at nice hotels? We do these things because we all like to be taken care of, don't we? As a matter of fact, we're willing to pay dearly for it, doling out plenty for first class seats on planes, room upgrades at hotels, and domestic help to come into our homes to clean.

Let me ask you, would you rather sail to the Cayman Islands in a row boat or on a luxury liner? I thought so. Me too!

Now let's take a look at another key component in the *Taming Tigers* method, an essential principle that works hand-in-hand with relationship-building: Communication.

Dan Stockdale

NOTES

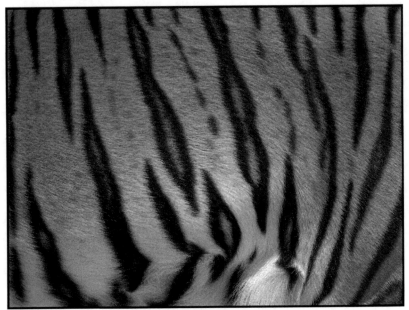

Tiger stripes are like finger prints. Every tiger has their very own unique pattern.

Chapter 11: Taming Tigers Secret #3

Communication

> *"Would people value having a colleague say "Thank You" and "Good Job"? I thought about how I would feel – and I realized the incredible power of recognizing and appreciating others."*
> *-Andris Ramans, Intuitive Surgical*

I told you in the last chapter that the easiest and best way to figure out what someone's needs are is not to *figure* at all but to *ask* them. Similarly, training others in relationship-building, particularly encouraging them to practice altruism, involves training them to *ask*.

Tigers in the wild tell others they're in the area by marking territory: spraying surrounding trees and bushes with urine, droppings that are prominently placed, and leaving deep scratch marks on tree trunks. Very little communication between tigers is vocal.

Asking is just one important aspect of communication, and communication is essential in order to tame your tigers.

Many of us believe that communication skills are somehow innate, that you either have them or you don't. This isn't true. Using

Dan Stockdale

Taming Tigers Techniques, you can learn to communicate better –
even brilliantly – in order to achieve the behaviors you want from
others. 3Ts will help you to improve communication in all its aspects.

Communication Among Trainers
Communication among animal trainers and caretakers is an ongoing
process that occurs frequently throughout the day. After cleaning
enclosures, trainers communicate with each other about any
indications they found that would point toward problems with an
animal's physical function. Trainers communicate verbally and in
writing.

Trainers communicate with each other daily about training progress
on behaviors that are being learned. How long was spent training?
How many repetitions? What was the response? What type of
reinforcement?

Trainers communicate with each other about their observations of
each animal's behavior. They also observe interactions between
animals to look for any untoward signs of conflict between the
animals. Yes, animals, just like humans, sometimes have personality
clashes.

Communication is the vital link between trainers that provides
assurance that the animals in their care are receiving the best possible
treatment.

You're Like Dr. Doolittle Communicating with the Animals!
We all know communication is important; we are told so all the time
by speakers at conferences, books and magazines, talk show hosts
and, occasionally, our beloved significant others. Why all the chatter
about communication? So many people still preach about the need
for good communication because many of us still haven't caught on.

I, for one, find that I am not perfect in the communication department
with humans, though I strive constantly. At times, I do a far better job

communicating with the animals I work with than with humans, so let me first give you some examples of that.

When trainers have a young animal to raise - say, a baby monkey or a tiger cub - they begin developing familiarity and bonds; they establish a relationship, as we discussed in the last chapter. You may have done this with a household pet, bringing Fido home, for example, and petting him, making sure he has a nice soft bed to lie in, feeding him, and giving him toys; your spouse may even let Fido sleep in your bed with you (although my wife drew the line when I tried to bring a baby monkey to bed. I guess everyone has their limits!)

Back to Fido, you begin communicating by developing familiarity and a bond with the animal. Before you know it, you can tell when that little puppy needs to go outside. Sure, there are accidents, and that's okay. It's just like when the tiger cub chews off the leg of the antique couch that's been in your wife's family for 100 years. That's okay…er, maybe not!

But the bottom line is that you and your puppy are learning each other's habits and routines. You're learning that, after you have fed and watered Fido, it's a good idea to take him for a walk to avoid an accident on the carpet. And Fido learns, too. He learns that after he eats, you generally walk him to the door, and then you go out the door, and then he takes care of business, and then you praise him with exuberance! You might even give him a puppy treat if he takes care of *both* toileting functions!

Before you know it, Fido goes over to the door and barks when he wants to go out. What do you know - *bidirectional* communication is taking place! You learn and Fido learns.

What is the correlation of all this to your communications with human animals? Well, first, sometimes you have to expect and tolerate a lot of little "accidents" before you and the person you're trying to communicate with get the hang of things.

Second, communication doesn't have to be verbal. Many times, actually most of the time, our non-verbals speak *volumes* more than our actual words. Have you ever had a friend, significant other, or coworker where you knew what each other thought without saying a word?

The First Stripe of Communication: Creating and Earning Mutual Respect
The first step (or stripe!) toward great communication is sincerely showing that you care, that you're engaged in the process, and that you desire to communicate. To accomplish this, mutual respect is essential.

> The first stripe of communication is sincerely showing that you care.

Good communication arises not from fear but from mutual respect. Fear stifles and muddles communication, while respect breaks such barriers down. When those you work for, and those who work for you, feel your respect for them, they come to respect you. 3Ts has the Golden Rule as one of its roots: treat others – *all* others – as you would like to be treated.

Remember, behavior breeds behavior. If you expect others to respect you, you must first respect them. You show respect to others by doing the right thing and by telling the truth, even when it hurts.

How do you earn respect? You earn it by *giving* it. It is a self-perpetuating cycle of the best sort. As a leader, people watch you. They also follow your lead in their behavior. If you are disrespectful to or speak badly of the employees who work in the employee cafeteria, I will guarantee your staff will feel at liberty to do the same. If, however, you respect them, those you lead will probably act the same way.

- *You earn respect by honoring your word.* If you say you are going to do something, you *must* do it. You don't have a choice, assuming of course that you've not made a promise that's illegal, immoral or unethical, in which case you shouldn't have ever offered to do it in the first place!

- *You earn respect by making the right decisions*, even when they're not popular or in your personal best interest. For example, if your payroll department discovers an error in an employee's paycheck – they've been overcharging for dental premiums – the easy (but wrong) decision would be to say: "We'll correct it going forward." The more difficult (but right) thing to say is: "We will correct it retroactively to when the error first occurred, and refund the difference, with interest."

The Second Stripe of Communication: What's in it for Them?
I was working with another trainer, watching him as he trained a young hyena to come back to us on command. We were in a canyon and letting the hyena venture away from us a few feet. Then, we would sound a buzzer, the hyena would run back, and she would get a treat. Then we would let her go further, sound the buzzer, and she would return. We kept increasing the distance, and she would always return when she heard the sound of the buzzer. We even let her get halfway up the side of the canyon, way out of sight in the surrounding scrub brush, yet, when we sounded the buzzer, she would come running, a treat would be produced, and she would bounce around happily for a few moments, then make her way out on another adventure.

> The second stripe of communication is having the right payoff.

What does payoff have to do with communication? You must look at the communication process from the other person's perspective. Know *what is in it for them*. In our hyena example, the tasty morsel was the "what is in it for me."

So, what is in it for your "tigers"? Are the only words they hear harsh and demanding, or do they hear words of concern? Make sure your words motivate those around you to *want* to communicate!

Dan Stockdale

You have to understand why the other partner in the communication process is listening to you. What is their motivation or pay-off? Maybe your employees listen because they *have* to, because of your position. Or, worse yet, do you use fear to motivate? Wouldn't it be better for you and for them if they listened because they *wanted* to?

The Third Stripe of Communication: Get the Proper Training
When I decided to start working with large cats, I sought out the proper training. I began by visiting several facilities. I asked questions. I interviewed other trainers. I spent three weeks in the desert with daytime temperatures never dropping below 105 degrees in a structured program that was designed to teach all aspects of handling and husbandry of exotic animals. I learned about the myriad of international, federal, state and local guidelines.

You may be thinking, "I've been communicating all of my life. Why do I need training? I can talk!"

> The third stripe of communicating with tigers is to get the appropriate

Please understand that talking does not equal communicating. The mere fact that you utter words doesn't necessarily mean that what's in your head is being absorbed by the other party effectively. We often assume that our words will land with the intended message, but we're frequently wrong. With training, however, we can better the odds considerably.

Training in communication is essential in order to excel at 3Ts. If you write articles for the company's employee newsletter, a college level course in business writing might just be the ticket you need to polish up your written communication skills.

If one aspect of your work is presenting at meetings large or small, a session or two with a presentation coach might be in order. If your communication is primarily one on one, try immersing yourself in an interpersonal communication class.

172

The Fourth Stripe of Communication: Have the Right Equipment
To communicate in animal training, we might use equipment like the buzzer I mentioned with the hyena. With many animals, especially marine animals, trainers use a whistle to communicate. With large cats, trainers frequently use a fiberglass feed stick to "pay" an animal its reward. This piece of equipment also aids in safety in that you don't have to actually put your hand to the mouth of the tiger in order to present a reward. Pretty good idea, huh?

> The fourth stripe of communication is having the right equipment.

Yet another piece of equipment used is a communication stick, a piece of rattan anywhere from 18" to 30" long. An extension of the trainer's hand, the stick allows the animal to see commands more easily from a distance. For example, if I point to a spot on the ground with my finger and say "go to mark" (go to the spot I am pointing to), it is much harder for the animal to see where I'm pointing if all I'm using is a 4" finger. If, however, I point with a 24" communication stick, it's far easier for the animal to see the mark and obey the command.

Trainers always try to keep their communication sticks between themselves and the part of the tiger that can do the most damage: the mouth. For example, when standing beside a tiger, I will simply hold the stick at my side between the tiger and me. In actuality, it's not much of a barrier, but the cats have been trained to think of the stick as a barrier and know that they're not supposed to go past it.

Of course, everyone has their own training style and not all trainers use a communication stick. Some rely purely on their relationship and verbal commands to tell the animal where to go and what to do.

Your communication 'tools' may be monthly board meetings, your computer, your voice, a microphone, one-on-one meetings with managers, a website, or a blog. If you're a CEO set to speak to the annual shareholders' meeting, you had better make sure you're very comfortable with the microphone you're using before you emerge in front of the crowd with a screeching microphone squealing with feedback. Also, what kind of microphone are you going to use? Are you more comfortable with a handheld or a lavaliere?

Or, maybe your communication tool is a computer. Whatever the tools you pick when you communicate, be sure you have the right equipment for the communication task at hand. And, be sure you are using those tools in the most effective manner possible.

The Fifth Stripe of Communication: Can You Hear Me Now?
When working with a large cat like a tiger, trainers must listen carefully and at all times, especially to the backup trainer, who is right beside the cat holding the leash. He or she is the one in closest proximity to the cat and is the most in tune with what the animal is feeling moment-by-moment.

In your jungle, who's watching your back for you? Do you have a team that you listen to and that you can count on to watch your tigers? Who comprises your team of "backup trainers"? Do you have enough confidence in them to trust them with your life?

> The fifth stripe of communication is listening actively.

There is more to communication than just clearly articulating what you need. It's equally important to listen well and to follow through on what you learn from those you communicate with. You can have all the potential in the world for real success, but unless you are able to express yourself clearly, listen actively, and take meaningful action, you will never achieve the level of success that you deserve and *could* attain.

The Sixth Stripe of Communication: Coming in Clearly
When training tigers, clarity is an essential aspect of communication. If I signal the cat to sit up, I am careful to be very definitive and clear with my signals so that the cat sees it and knows that I am signaling

the command "Up." If I am not giving clear signals, I can't blame the tiger for not producing the behavior I requested. He or she does not understand what I am "saying." This holds true for auditory and visual stimuli as well. When you are cuing the tiger, you must make sure your communication is clear and consistent.

> The sixth stripe of communication is clarity.

As I said, tiger trainers always have a back-up trainer assisting them with big cats. So, not only is clarity important with your animal, it's important with your backup trainer - your team. If I ask my backup to take the tiger we're working with to a holding area for a break, we take extreme care in exercising clarity in our communication. If I tell the assistant that I will open the gate, and he thinks I said "Wait," but the tiger hears "gate," then *everyone* is confused.

In our work lives, we must also clearly express precisely what we need, in every interaction. Those with whom you interact deserve to have clarity in your communication with them. If you're not unmistakably communicating your needs and expectations to those in your tribe, and striving for clarity when they communicate, you can't expect positive, productive results.

Too, if the administrators of the various tiger preserves around the world are not communicating with clarity with each other, the very existence of a species in the wild will be in serious danger.

If the tiger population counts are not performed consistently and accurately from one preserve to another, as was recently asserted by an Asian newspaper, it could have devastating effects.

If your administrators are not communicating well within your organization, you, too, could face extinction before you know it. Conservation of our endangered species and your business is not an *option*, it's a principled *obligation*.

175

Dan Stockdale

Well, if we are communicating with our tigers properly by using the Seven Stripes of Communication, we next need to consider a deeper exploration of the concept of Motivation.

NOTES

A marmoset hanging out with one of its favorite foods - a banana!

Chapter 12: Taming Tigers Secret #4

Motivation

> *"If you can create a community that supports itself,*
> *you can really achieve wonderful things."*
> *-Keith Sonberg, Roche Bioscience*

Have you ever sat in a movie and watched the animals on screen, wondering how they were able to get the animals to do the behaviors you see? Or have you ever gone to the circus and watched the animal acts and wondered how they could get the animals to perform those feats on cue?

If you have, you have seen the end result of a complex puzzle called motivation. Somewhere, trainers have spent time with each animal and figured out what "reinforcer" would motivate it to do the desired behaviors. Then, they have used that reinforcer to train the animal to deliver the behaviors.

If you have ever tried to get people to do something they didn't want to do – and who hasn't been in *that* position? - you probably quickly realized that it's a difficult, if not impossible, proposition. No one wants to be forced or manipulated, and neither people nor animals will do anything for long that they really don't want to do.

But what if whatever they *don't* want to do becomes something they *do* want to do?

Think of it as the Tom Sawyer phenomenon: Remember the story about him having to paint the fence? He convinced all of his friends to help him by making it seem like the most fun they could ever possibly hope to have! Having a good time is an excellent motivator. Both animals and people *want* to have fun and desire to perform well.

What's in Your Bait Bag?
To successfully influence the behavior of others, you must find ways to stroke them, to *motivate* them and offer those motivations – primary and secondary reinforcers – consistently and repeatedly.

What motivates you may not motivate me, and what motivates me may not motivate other people, so you need to find out what works to influence each individual. For example, many people work for the money, while some work so they can have health insurance. Others work to ensure a financially secure retirement. And still others work simply because they enjoy the perks; I know of retirees who work for airlines just so they can travel for free.

What motivates a 22-year-old college graduate is probably going to be far different from what motivates a part-time 70-year-old retired executive who just wants to be around people.

And, to take it a step further, some people actually *volunteer* their time at meaningful labor, working without pay for *personal satisfaction*, motivated by the desire to *make a difference*. Money, insurance, benefits and retirement income don't mean a thing to them. But they will work their tails off by donating 20 or 30 hours of their time a week just to get a lapel pin at the annual hospital volunteer banquet that honors their service.

Motivation and Consistency with Big Cats

To train tigers, timing is everything. You always have to keep in mind *what* you're reinforcing and the timing of reward must be the *same way, every time.* If a trainer gives the command to a tiger to "Sit," and delivers the command and the reward quickly and consistently, the animal will learn the behavior much quicker. Of course there will be slight variations, but the goal is to reinforce (or bridge) the behavior within a fraction of a second from when the behavior occurred.

For this technique to be successful, I must be very clear about what behavior I am rewarding. For example, if I give an animal the command to sit, and she sits, then looks off to the side to see what is going on over on the hillside, *then* she gets the reward, she is been rewarded for looking to the hillside, not for sitting.

The animal learns like this: "If every time I do what he says, I get this little chunk of meat, I will do what he says in order to get the chunk of meat." That's really not complicated, is it? Depending upon how quickly an animal is learning, within minutes, a trainer can begin to build the sitting behavior in response to the "Sit" command in conjunction with the reward. But trainers must be careful. If sometimes the tiger gets the chunk of meat after sitting, then glancing at the hillside, or sitting, then looking down to the ground to see what just ran across, or sitting, then yawning, the trainer has reinforced hillside glancing, ground-gazing, and yawning, not sitting. Which means it will take the trainer longer to get to the behavior of sitting. The animal understandably thinks what is being rewarded is whatever behavior immediately preceded the reward.

So, what's in *your* bait bag?

Here is another example: We train birds to do what we call an "eagle," which is where they hold out their wings for display, like an eagle in flight. To get this behavior, a trainer has the bird perched on his or her arm. Then the trainer turns her arm ever so slightly, and the bird spreads its wings out as it balances and prepares to take flight. Each time the bird reaches the furthest point of the spread, the trainer rewards the bird until the wings are spread all the way back to a full display. But if the trainer attains a full eagle spread, and the bird flies off over to another perch, and *then* gets its reward…you get the idea.

Meat Chunks and Praise: Primary and Secondary Reinforcers for Animals

Sometimes tigers do behaviors for their trainers simply because they want to please them. Pleasing the trainer (and the resulting scratches behind the ears) is, in this case, what is known as a "secondary reinforcer." But, the food the trainers offer the tigers is the primary force that motivates them to perform, so it is known as a "primary reinforcer," because it is necessary to the animals survival.

Why does an animal do a behavior for a trainer? Because they want a primary or secondary reinforcer. Primary reinforcers generally are the strongest means to achieve the quickest behavior. With tigers, that is raw chunks of meat; they will almost always work for food, which is highly motivating to them.

For animals, the reward for a behavior does not *have* to be a chunk of meat. Secondary reinforcers are not necessarily *less* motivating or less sought-after rewards, but they are not needed for the animal's survival. Secondary reinforcers tell animals that they have done a good job, but the animals' desire for them is not biologically motivated.

Secondary reinforcers are verbal and physical strokes, a mix of encouraging words and touch: pats on the head, belly rubs, and lots of "Good job! Good girl!" talk. Motivation for a tiger, then, can be a combination of primary reinforcers (food), secondary reinforces (stokes down the back), and a desire to please the trainer.

Money and "Attaboys": Primary and Secondary Reinforcers for People

What do you think the primary reinforcer is for people at work? That's pretty easy, right? Money. Most of us need a paycheck to survive; that is our raw chunks of meat. But people, like animals, also respond well to verbal "strokes" and "Attaboys," and these can powerfully influence behavior.

You can do a lot of things to people at work; you can change their work hours, change their job duties, or even relocate their offices. But when you start messing with their paychecks, look out! This primary reinforcement is near and dear to the hearts of those who receive one and will cause snarling and growling if anyone does mess with it.

People usually want to please those they care about in their personal relationships, and in business, most people want to do a good job so that they can be proud of their accomplishments and have job security. For people, these secondary reinforcers are frequently just as important as the primary motivators like money.

Aside from money for survival, and a pat on the back, what else are people working for? What motivates them? Maybe one person wants to work part-time or work from home so they can spend more time with their kids, so a motivator is a flexible schedule. Another person, highly-motivated to move up the career ladder, could be motivated by added responsibilities that allow a quicker climb. Another might want more time off in the spring to coach his or her child's Little League games. The possibilities are as endless and as individual as we humans.

Secondary reinforcement provides a feeling of fulfillment, not necessarily a monetary reward or something to fill the stomach. As with animals, one type of reinforcement is not necessarily better than another, but there must be balance, and what works will be different for different people.

Now, let's do an exercise. Write down the names of the individuals in your personal and professional tribes. Then beside each name write down a secondary reinforcer for each person. Do you know what motivator those in your tribe prefer?

Reinforcers to Get Your Employees Performing!
Organizations may mistakenly fail to realize the need for
reinforcement balance, assuming that the primary reinforcer of the
paycheck should be enough to motivate every employee. I have
actually heard VP's say this, and whenever I hear it, I cringe inside
because I instantly know that this person does not understand how to
use motivation within the organization to achieve maximum results
for the company and shareholders.

Let me give you an example. I know a woman whose husband passed
away and left her in extremely good financial shape. She does not
have to work, but she chooses to because she wants something to do
and wants to make a contribution to her community. In the workplace,
money is not a motivator for her like it is for most people. But
because she lost her spouse of many years, she is very lonely and in
need psychologically. Positive verbal reinforcement, the 'Attaboys',
means the world to her.

Sincere praise can be an excellent motivator. Both animals and
humans need to know that *you* know they're making progress if you
want to motivate them to continue moving forward. So, rather than
bellowing about "bad" behaviors, *praise the good ones*, and you will
find it improves performance and relationships.

Using Repetition in Motivation
In training animals, repetition is crucial to their success in learning a
behavior. You probably know this from teaching your own pets basic
obedience. If you tell a puppy to "Sit" as its rump is sitting down, you
may get it to show that behavior again, or you may not.

But practice it for 5 minutes every morning and another 5 minutes
every evening, and you will have a champion sitter before you can
say "Good boy!"

In business, repetition can reinforce desired behaviors and teach new behaviors, too. Repetition enhances motivation when you find processes that work and do them the same way every time.

> Repetition is crucial to success in training animals and office "tigers" too.

Repetition is itself a motivating factor. Many of us take pleasure in the feeling of accomplishment we get when we successfully complete a project. As we repeatedly complete a task, as we replicate the task successfully again and again, we are increasing our motivation to perform the task the next time. We are also making the task routine, a good habit if you will.

For example, if your divisional managers' monthly reports for the prior month are due on the second Friday of each month, they will come to repetitively turn them in on that day with a little practice, motivation, and repetition.

Now, can you imagine the confusion it would cause if this repetitive pattern was broken because you called them all on the first Friday of the month and screech at them for not having their reports in on time.

Why would the untimely call bring about a decrease in motivation and a resulting hiccup in the divisional manager's repetition of the task? The reason is that it adds confusion into the equation. Although change *can* be good, it does in fact cause some level of confusion. And random, inexplicable change adds further to the confusion factor. Adding confusion into the motivation and repetition equation will almost always cause performance attributes and desired behavior to decrease.

Establishing a Reward Schedule
After identifying what primary and secondary reinforcers will work for a particular individual, whether that individual is a spotted leopard or an employee with a checkered past, you must determine what type of "reward schedule" to set up.

Dan Stockdale

A reward schedule involves which rewards you're going to give, when you're going to give them, and in what amount. For example, most employees get a primary reinforcer in the form of their paycheck. That paycheck pays them a specific thing (money), in a specific amount (the hourly wage) on a specific schedule (every two weeks). So, this is a *fixed* type of reward, a specific amount occurring repeatedly at a set interval. Basically, it rewards them for showing up.

Keep in mind, however, there are also variable reward schedules. An example of a variable reward would be a sales commission. If your commission is 5% and you sell $1000 worth of product this week, you will earn $50. If you sell $10,000 worth of product you will earn $500. If you sell nothing, you earn, well, nothing.

Accentuating the Positive as Motivation
Sales provides excellent examples of the differences between positive and negative reinforcers. Even if you have never been in sales yourself, you probably know someone who has, and you know that they're more often negatively reinforced – when their numbers aren't there – than they are positively reinforced when their numbers are great.

If Karen's quota is twenty units per month, and on the 25th of the month she has only sold three units, her manager is almost certainly going to focus on the units that *aren't* sold, perhaps "motivating" her with ambiguous (or not so ambiguous) threats to her future employment like, "You know what happened to George when he didn't meet *his* quota for 90 days. I'd hate it if you ended up like him."

What if, instead, the manager sincerely praised her for the three units she has sold and then asked, "Okay, what can we do to help you? How did you get the three sales you made? Maybe you won't get to quota this month, but what can we do so that we can get a head start on *next* month? Let's look at your leads!"

Being flexible here wouldn't mean adjusting the quota so that she could reach it; 3TS are never about lowering the bar. While Karen might appreciate that, such an action wouldn't be motivating in the long term and would have a negative impact on the bottom line.

Practicing 3Ts, her manager would find out what, aside from fear, would really motivate Karen to sell as much or more than is required of her. "What is it going to take to get you there?" and "What help do you need?" are questions that will yield positive results and show the manager what hands-on approach will yield the sought-after outcome. A question like "How can I help you achieve the goal?" may be met with astonishment from a more seasoned salesperson, used to the threats and abuse of some sales jobs, or complete bewilderment from those who are new to the job.

If you're training this manager in 3Ts, you might suggest positive comments like, "Maybe your training hasn't been as complete as it could be, and you're not totally comfortable closing sales yet. Why don't I ride along with you and help you with your calls?"

The intention here can't be, "I am going to look over your shoulder, see what you are doing wrong, and nail you for it when we get back to the office." The option must be presented sincerely and with an intention to motivate, or such a positive offer becomes an insincere negative one, and integrity flies out the window faster than a red-tailed hawk on the hunt. Efforts to improve a salesperson's training and performance can be perceived as punishment if not handled properly by the leader.

Rewarding Specific Behaviors with Bonuses
Regular paychecks aren't always the world's greatest motivator. Sure, everyone wants the money, but think for a minute: what did the company reward you for? Was it the report you turned in last week? Or was it the number of new, qualified sales leads you produced this week? Or was it because you handled an irate customer well? Was it because you are a warm body who filled a position, and they think you're working? Who knows?

Frankly, you probably weren't rewarded for *any* of those behaviors. Hopefully, your accomplishments were appreciated, but the reward was too far past the point of any specific behavior for you to know if any of those behaviors were reinforced. You probably received a check because you're an employee, employees get checks, you showed up for work, and so you "earned" it.

If a customer service call center employee who handles 3 calls per hour is compensated the same as one who handles 10 calls per hour, what's the motivation to improve? There isn't any.

You may have surmised by my tone that I am a fanatical advocate of bonus systems. That way, you know what you're working toward; you know the goal.

Loosen Up: Motivating Ourselves to Motivate
While you may agree with me that a million different things motivate people, you may still be unable to figure out how to make this idea work for you. Sometimes *determining* what motivates people is not nearly as difficult as getting ourselves to *implement* individualized rewards.

For example, it's very easy to say, "Well, I can't let Jim come in at 6:00 and get off at 3:00 to meet his kids' bus because then everyone else would want off at 3:00, too." You may think you're practicing a policy of consistency – which I advocate, right? But saying, "If I do it for you, I have to do it for everyone" comes from *rigidity*, not consistency.

If *I* was your employee, it would not be very motivating for me to "be there for the bus." Although I like to be with my son every possible minute, my son drives himself to and from school, so I don't have the same need as the parent of an elementary school student.

However, if you were my boss, I would ask you if I could bring my pet to work. Progressive companies sometimes allow this perk. Of course, before you say "Yes" to me, you would be wise to ask what kind of pet I have. Most people would bring a dog. Me? I would bring a monkey, macaw, or maybe even a tiger cub! Could you be flexible enough to motivate me with this secondary reinforcer? (Psssst. If you hire me, we'll keep the tiger under the desk our little secret, okay? And by all means, whatever you do, don't tell Risk Management. There are some things they just don't need to know!)

Motivation and Consistency
There are various types of rewards and reward schedules. The trick is to figure out what will work with each individual tiger in your world. Thus, motivation and consistency of reinforcement are intrinsically tied together.

Leaders must be fair and consistent if they hope to keep employees motivated, energized, and positively reinforced. As with animals, people have a need for consistency in order to learn, and indeed in order to function.

> Leaders must be fair and consistent if they hope to keep employees motivated, energized, and positively reinforced.

You have undoubtedly experienced firsthand how ridiculously difficult it can be to deal with people when you have no idea from one minute to the next how they will behave. You may also know how hard it is to do a good job when one day you're recognized and rewarded for your work and the next day you're criticized and told that you're doing a poor job. Trust me: your work did not change; your "judge" did.

Even if you have not had this experience in the workplace, you probably have seen it in a relationship of some other kind. It's easy to see how someone would not want to deal for long with the pressure of an erratic boss, partner, or other relationship. So you must work diligently so that *you* are not that boss or partner. You must practice consistency!

Roy's HR nightmare

Consistency can be tougher to practice than you might think. Let's spend a few minutes with Roy, a senior staff member for a governmental entity.

When Roy was first hired, he was given the task of rewriting the city's employee handbook. The one being used in 2007 had been written in the 1970s and though it had received a few revisions and updates over the years, he was amazed at how antiquated the language and policies were as set forth in the handbook. Hundreds of employees and dozens of department managers were all distributing the outdated guide.

If you've ever had to write an employee handbook, especially for a government entity, you know that it's a painstaking process to do properly. There are local, state, and federal laws to be followed, prior precedents, political favors that have been granted over the years. It's a real chore to accomplish.

Well, once the handbook was written, Roy had his supervisor review the document. In addition, he had his subordinates who were involved in management review it, too. Even the city's personnel committee and the city commissioners reviewed it and unanimously approved it as one of the best works, one of the most thorough documents, they had seen.

Upon completion of the process, he handed the implementation phase over to the director of Human Resources. Lo and behold, after the new employee handbook was unveiled, and hundreds of employees were in-serviced on its contents, some managers implemented disciplinary action for attendance issues, and some did not. Some managers gave preferential treatment to employees who were friends of city commissioners, and some did not. Some managers read and learned the policies, and some did not. After hundreds of hours of work, and tens of thousands of dollars in training expense, they still were unable to achieve consistency.

It appears that in this city's scenario, the training took place merely for the sake of training. The great handbook notwithstanding, there was a breakdown in discerning what would *motivate* managers to implement with consistency the revised handbook's policies.

Using Motivation to Make Things Right
So, what would have been an alternative for our frustrated HR Director? How about a contest between departments with each team getting points for knowing and applying the policies in the new handbook? Or, group meetings with all managers where they implement a policy-a-day? There are a thousand and one motivators that may have worked here, as long as they were applied consistently.

Maybe your personal issue with consistency is that your boss treats your peers differently than you. Maybe you're the one who needs to experience consistency in motivation from someone else. How do you handle a boss who plays favorites, whether intentionally or unintentionally?

Well, let's go back a few pages and start with communication. Maybe you can sit down with your supervisor and discuss your concerns. Think it through and give your boss some credit for being a decent human being. Maybe the inconsistency was unintentional; he or she may actually be grateful if you point out the problem.

If you're not comfortable with the direct communication approach, you could approach your concerns incrementally. If, for example, you know someone you work with is receiving preferential treatment on vacation requests, you could send your boss an email asking *in a non-threatening manner* how to interpret the vacation policy so that you will know for your future requests. The key here is *non-threatening*. Your goal here is to tame a tiger, not infuriate one!

Maybe something that you are unaware of has motivated the inconsistent behavior. Try to figure out what is motivating your bosses actions. Something is and it's your tiger to figure out. Please keep in mind that I'm not saying it's fair and I'm not saying that it's the way it should be. But sometimes we have to work with situations that simply aren't evenhanded.

Of course, there are other ways to approach the situation but you get the idea. You can't lie down and let the inconsistencies continue. You must develop a personal style that will allow you to address issues in a professional manner.

Seek Motivational Flexibility, not Rigidity

Taking a rigid, cookie-cutter approach to business is an excuse to not innovate or progress. Structure for the sake of structure is ultimately pointless and fruitless. Business, especially at the upper levels of corporate America, is traditionally all about the numbers: concrete, objective, measurable black-and-white numbers that let us measure our success with an easily understood and quantified benchmark.

So, what does this have to do with motivation? Structure and rigidity can be the death of motivation. Finding the right balance is essential.

Although structure may be useful at the top, no matter how much we might wish it so, business at the lower echelons actually operates in a world of *gray*, not within strict black-and-white lines. So, if it doesn't adversely affect the business to be flexible in terms of scheduling, or other things that actually allow you to use your power to have a positive impact on the lives of your employees, there really is no reason NOT to do it, is there?

Of course Human Resources and legal departments prefer the traditional black-and-white model. They want everything to be the same for everyone, and I understand: This rigidity theoretically makes it easier for them to defend the organization against grievances or legal battles.

Strictly speaking, they're right. However, significant legal battles over minute issues are rare. Yes, they can be brought into bigger picture issues, but they are rarely seen as the single focus of major litigation.

When you find yourself in a situation that has little or no potential for future litigation if you adjust your policy - when adjusting it will open up a reinforcer that will motivate one or more employees - *be flexible*. Make it your *policy* to consider things on a case-by-case basis. It goes without saying – but to keep the legal department happy I will say it anyway - that you must ensure that you are being fair and not violating any laws or showing differential treatment to protected classes.

> Structure and rigidity can be the death of motivation. Finding the right balance is essential.

Consistently Apply Policies

You'll notice the word "balance" shows up quite often in this book; it's an essential ingredient in 3Ts. Being consistent in the way you apply your policies can be a real balancing act. Human nature causes us to push limits and test boundaries.

Animals do it, too. When I walk into an enclosure with an animal, the animal immediately starts sizing me up. It wants to see what I'm made of. Do I cower back slightly? Do I act apprehensive? Or, do I walk in with too much self-confidence, so that I'm perceived as a threat? I'll be evaluated no matter what approach I take.

People size each other up, too, evaluating what others are made of. Leaders of all kinds need to be fair, firm, and flexible, and they need to realize their boundaries, and then enforce those boundaries consistently.

It's only fair: While you must remain flexible when working with individuals to meet their needs – such as adjusting an employee's schedule to allow him or her to meet family obligations – doing so in the service of positive motivation doesn't mean you must abandon the consistent application of policies.

There's no sense in throwing out the cub with the bathwater by abandoning all policies in an effort to be totally flexible. If that employee whose schedule you adjusted – or *any* employee, including management – is late three times, and your employee handbook says that three tardies warrants a verbal warning, you must be consistent and issue that warning.

If you are to be consistent, all the leaders in your organization must be consistent, too. And if anyone's idea of "consistent" means being consistently late to work, then you have a problem, and you need to fairly apply the policy to remedy it.

Maybe that late employee has a problem at home that is affecting her work. Or, she may be lying when she tells you that she has personal issues that cause the tardiness; she may simply be testing you to see what she can get away with, believing that if you were flexible enough to adjust her hours, you might not notice that she is coming in late every now and then. In spite of your best efforts at flexibility, *her* behavior still dictates that you apply the organization's policies in disciplining her.

In that sort of situation, if I have been flexible and done my part, I am no longer concerned about *why* the employee is noncompliant. At that point, by further trying to meet her needs, I would just be enabling her and allowing her to continue to take advantage of the situation. I must achieve *balance* between flexibility and consistency so that everyone knows that attempts to push the boundaries just for the sake of pushing them will not work.

Next, let's take a look at other principles to help you tame your tigers, perception and awareness.

TIGER TALKING POINTS

1. What "tools" did tiger tamers formerly use?

2. What "tools" do we use now?

3. What experiment did Thorndike use to test operant conditioning?

4. Which is reinforced: the organism or the organisms' response?

5. What is positive reinforcement?

6. What is extinction?

7. Is it ever wise for tigers to view you as passive? Why or why not?

Tigers spend from 14 - 18 hours a day dozing and sleeping.

Chapter 13: Taming Tigers Principle #5

Perception and Awareness

> *"There are no shortages of opportunities for people to do great things. They can, and they must."*
> *-Mary Beth Cahill-Phillips, Trustline*

Are you perceptive? Or are you projective? Have you ever thought about the difference?

Are you able to look "into" others and see what's really going on? Or do you tend to "project" your own feelings, ideas, and behaviors onto others, seeing only what you feel they *should* or *may* be doing or feeling, in your opinion?

Skilled animal trainers learn to be willing and able to read an animal and to be open enough for the animal to read them right back. Perception is a two-way street, and both participants must be in tune with the other's disposition.

This level of reciprocal perception and awareness is essential to the trainer-animal relationship, just as it is for you to have successful relationships and achieve the behaviors you want from those in your own life.

Mutual Perception in Tiger Training

A tiger needs to perceive its trainer's strength, too, so when it enters an arena, ballroom, or soundstage, everyone should stand. In this way, the tiger perceives the strength of each person there as well as the strength of the group as a whole.

When trainers work with a tiger in close proximity to individuals who aren't accustomed to being around big cats, we always give a safety talk to advise those individuals how to act both individually and collectively should the animal get loose. We teach them to stay together if the animal is loose so that it sees the strength of the gathered group.

There are numerous examples of the nuances of perception in the relationship of individual animals to their trainers. For example, trainers never work with tigers unless they feel 100% well. They never go into the arena with an animal if they are feeling even a little "off" because tigers read their trainer's body language and know if they are feeling uneasy.

Trainers don't expect this same level of perception from their human counterparts, so they know to speak up to their teammates if they feel apprehensive – good communication is Principle #3, remember – rather than trying to hide it from them and endangering everyone. Trainers learn quickly that they can't hide any hesitant feelings from a tiger. Tigers can perceive confidence, and they can perceive fear. When trainers lack confidence, nothing good is going to come of their interaction with the animal.

People Perceive Blustering Bullies, Too

An inexperienced trainer may actually attempt to overcompensate and try to make himself appear more confident than he actually is. Maybe you know people who behave this way with others on the job or in social environments – grown-up bullies trying to hide their insecurities by barking and blustering their way through relationships. Just as it was on the playground, a grown-up bully, once confronted with an equally aggressive opponent, will turn his or her aggression elsewhere.

Or maybe you have been this way yourself with your own tigers: you throw your weight around in an effort to appear intimidating and might even try to get in the first blow before anyone catches on that you are apprehensive.

Like animals, humans can readily perceive fear, even if it is disguised by swaggering pseudo-confidence. If they are not "on to it" yet, they will be. Getting in the first punch will not keep a passive-aggressive closet-coward from being devoured, like a pack of wild hyenas consuming a carcass, when that fear is exposed for what it really is.

Never Take Your Eyes off Your Tigers (Again)

When trainers learn to train tigers, the most often-repeated rule is "*Never* take your eyes off your tigers!" To understand how to train a tiger, you must first understand a tiger's natural, wild behavior and tendencies… and you must always know *exactly* where he is.

When trainers are in an enclosed area or an environment where they are working with tigers for an extended period of time, they not only keep an eye on their tigers, they also give them breaks. So during some periods, they are working on behaviors and at other times, the animal just lies around sleeping, relaxing, and enjoying the enrichment of a new experience. Especially during the non-work periods, it can be tempting to become slack and unaware of the possible present danger. Here especially, you must always keep your eyes on your tigers.

Tigers are perceptive: they *perceive* confidence and control or the lack of it. So trainers have to be perceptive, too, and *self*-aware. They must send out signals to their animals that the trainer is fully in charge and completely aware of everything that the tiger might perceive during their interaction.

Dan Stockdale

The tigers that trainers work with are generally hand-raised and familiar with people, but *they are still wild animals*, and we can't ever forget that. At the end of the day – at anytime - they can kill us. Trainers can't let their animals get behind them, and must always remain cognizant of their surroundings while simultaneously ignoring any distractions. Nothing can be allowed to remove focus from the tiger.

Nonetheless, I have seen trainers who become lackadaisical and comfortable with the animals – maybe they have worked with their tigers for months or years – and as soon as they take their eyes off the animals, the potential exists for mischievous, even grave behavior to start.

Never, ever, ever take your eyes off of your tigers!

Jonathan, a trainer I know, was not paying full attention while working in an enclosure with his cougar. The playful cat decided it would be fun to pin Jonathan to the ground. Though amusing for the cougar, this created a very real danger for Mark when he took his eye off of his "tiger."

Just recently, another friend of mine was caught not paying attention to the details. His insufficient awareness could have been disastrous. Because of the cold weather, he wore gloves while cleaning a tiger's enclosure from outside. He had one hand on the side of the enclosure as he sprayed it down, and the tiger, Tosha, saw it and thought, "Ooh! Toy!"

This trainer had worked with Tosha for years, and she is a great tiger, but she perceived that the glove was the trainer introducing an enrichment toy. In the spirit of play, she latched onto the glove, which happened to have his fingers in it. She gnawed on his gloved hand for about five minutes before she decided she was tired of playing with this new toy and finally opened her mouth. He was in the hospital for a few days with one of his fingers split down the middle, and another one half chewed off. Never, ever take your eyes off your tigers!

Keeping Your Eyes on Your "Tigers"

In the business world, your tigers will not necessarily attack you physically, but if you let your perception and awareness grow slack, your tigers can do irreparable harm. Whether your tiger is an issue or a person *you must always keep your eyes on that tiger.* Once you have identified your own tigers, you can't "back-burner" them or hope they will go away if you ignore them.

If you are operating a company where revenues are decreasing, and you have identified that tiger, it can be dangerously easy to get so wrapped up in handling operational issues and HR and physical plant issues, that you take your eye off your tiger of revenue. It need not be your *only* focus, just like trainers don't focus only on the tiger, but your tiger had better be your *primary* focus, or you are going to get bitten.

Of course, I am not saying that I expect you to be fully perceptive about your tigers every minute of every day. You may try, but realistically, there will be other things that will consume your time and energy unless you find yourself completely obsessed with one issue, and that's no good, either. It is a matter of *balance* again: You need to always keep your eyes open and remain alert, but not to the point of paranoia and obsession.

You must try to maintain constant awareness about what is going on around you in your environment. You want to be "mindful," rather than just coasting along with your fingers crossed, or over-focusing on one element of your life or one aspect of your business.

Perception and Problem-Solving

There is nothing magical about the fact that, when you focus on a problem, it seems to create energy that helps to solve the problem, or at least keep it in check. It's like learning to surf: The more time you devote to practicing, the better you will be and the easier it is.

One way to stay focused on *your* tiger is to actually enter its details in your calendar. Schedule a block of time every day that is specifically devoted to reviewing the issues surrounding your tiger.

If you have a problem with employee turnover in your organization, for example, schedule 15 minutes every day where you call any employees who quit in the past 24 hours. Ask them their thoughts. Sure, you will get some useless, tainted information, but you will also begin to see patterns developing. If they were stellar employees, find out about the possibilities of them returning. It may be "too little, too late," or it may just bring a star performer back to the team.

The mere fact that you are devoting time to looking at a problem is not necessarily going to solve it. You need to actually *do* something about it. If you are in healthcare, for example, and your tiger is poor patient care, it will not do much good to sit in your office and look at daily reports that offer further evidence of what you already know. You may have to conduct training. You may have to address issues with key managers. You may have to implement a motivation system that rewards the teams who have the greatest increase in customer service ratings. You will have to do something beyond simply allocating time to think about the problem. Remember, leadership is *action*.

Share What You See

Has there ever been someone in your life who has not done much to hide the fact that they resent you? Someone who seeks out or creates opportunities to undermine you and your authority? Someone whose lack of skills or poor attitude continually hampers your efforts to get the job done? If your 'tigers' are people whom you perceive as a threat, you want to always keep your eye on those individuals and what they are trying to accomplish.

Just as animal trainers document the behavior of the animals entrusted to them, you, too, must document actions, changes in behavior, altercations, and other information relevant to your tiger. Maintaining a journal is one of the best ways to ensure your survival when you're under attack.

When an animal trainer notices something unusual with an animal, she will follow through by notifying the appropriate individuals.

But when a tiger trainer notices something unusual with an animal, she doesn't stop at journaling the issue. She will also follow through by notifying the appropriate individuals. If she sees a tiger limping a bit after playing with a sibling, the trainer not only documents it but informs her supervisor or the veterinarian.

If your tigers are predatory humans, you need to watch your back and stay abreast of their activity so you know what they're saying and doing. As the saying goes, "Keep your friends close and your enemies even closer." If you're in a position organizationally superior to your tigers, it's obviously easier to keep a watch out and manage their workload to keep the focus on *your* priorities, not theirs.

When you perceive issues with a tiger, you're responsible for enlightening those who need to be informed about issues that are affecting or could affect the organization as well as your own self-preservation. I hasten to add that we're not talking about a first grade tattle-tale contest here, but as a professional you must inform others who have a need to know about a situation in a practiced, non-accusatory manner. Even if you aren't the tiger's supervisor, maintaining records and communicating the pertinent information is necessary.

Crouching Tiger, Hidden Tiger: Perceiving the Unknown
In addition to those tigers you may identify as you wander through your "jungle," you may discover that there are tigers lurking in the bushes that you don't see. These are people or issues that have the

potential to attack as soon as you let down your guard. They're ready to pounce, and you may not even know they are there. But if you stay flexible - *focused* but not rigid – you can be prepared to deal with those hidden tigers at a moment's notice.

I have encountered many hidden tigers in my life. It sometimes amazes me when I see the cruelty and lack of ethics in people's behavior. I have seen people brag about getting their peers fired. I have seen employees bake brownies for their boss with the main ingredient being a laxative (though this seemed funny at first, he ended up in the hospital.) I have seen highly regarded business people enter into agreements with trusted friends or colleagues with the sole intent of extracting every dollar they could from an unsuspecting and trusting "partner."

How do you deal with hidden tigers when you don't even know they're there? You can only perceive them by being constantly vigilant and by anticipating what potential dangers may lie in wait around the corner. No matter how much you trust someone, make sure that everything is *in writing* – including your exit strategy. Be aware of your surroundings and *anticipate* what could happen. Be perceptive. Be ever-alert. And always be thinking and planning ahead.

Learn From Your Tigers (and Leopards, too)
Tigers are not just potentially dangerous killing machines; they have much to teach their trainers. I will give you an example of what I mean using another big cat, Annie, a spotted leopard. Annie is so well-trained that if she doesn't get the reinforcement exactly when she thinks she should – if the trainers are just a second or two late in rewarding her – she hisses at them! She effectively tells us when she thinks we're slacking: "NOW is when you are supposed to give the reinforcement. NOW!" It doesn't take a super-perceptive trainer to pick up Annie's lessons on consistency. Give her the reinforcement meat on time and she's a doll. Delay it and she becomes a spotted grouch!

As I discussed earlier, one of the best ways to find out what your customers need is to simply *ask*, and then listen closely to what they tell you. Active listening is a form of perception, and if you listen to your tigers, they will provide you with needed information that wasn't obvious to you.

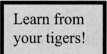

Observe your tigers' idiosyncrasies and be open to being coached by them. You will quickly learn things you might have had no other way of learning. If your tiger is an issue, rather than a person, is it likely to suddenly take on human traits and start talking to you? No. But through perception, awareness, and focus, you can gain the information you need to tame it.

Say you are the branch manager for a bank, and you want to know how to improve the public's impression of your service. Sit in the lobby for a few hours observing the traffic flow and the customers as they are waiting. Are they bored? Are they fidgeting? Are their children destroying the lobby one piece at a time? Would they obviously rather be somewhere else? How long are they standing?

What can you do to make the experience more pleasant? Learn from your tigers.

Defining Moments: Applying the Lessons of the Tigers to Constructive Change

You may be perceiving that the problem is actually *you*. If you've been operating in an overly negative environment – whether it's of your own making or not – and now you recognize the dilemma and want to create a more positive environment with 3Ts, you begin by creating a "defining moment": a time to tap into the strength of *complete* honesty about yourself which you share with an individual or your team.

The strength to be honest requires vulnerability. That may *seem* like a weakness, but those with whom you're candid will not perceive it that way. It takes real strength to speak the truth, especially about ourselves. So adjust the way you look at this idea, and give it a chance.

Start by acknowledging that you may have used an approach that could have been better in the past. If you want to make a fresh start, meet with the individual or group with whom you have been overly negative, and give some specific examples of where you believe you have chosen to take the a path that wasn't the best. Then say, "Going forward, I can't guarantee that I'll be perfect, but here are my goals, and this is what I am going to strive to do. I'm going to need to enlist your help to lend a hand in getting us there. If you see us veering off this new course, just gently nudge me and say so. I commit to doing likewise for you."

Can you see what you're doing here? You've *learned* from your tigers, applying your perception to problems to make a positive change that will have a constructive impact on the organization and its employees. You're building a team and creating cohesiveness. Maybe you're even asking your people to help train *you. This* is how you learn from your tigers!

Listen to your Tigers
Animal people learn over time what the normal sounds are for the animals within their care. After spending several days or weeks with the same critters you begin to notice certain patterns to their vocalizations. You get to know what's normal and what's not. Often you can tell if an animal is worried, scared, happy or playful just by the sounds you hear (or don't hear).

Listening is an often underused aspect of perception. Just as it's important for good communication, it's an invaluable tool to help you tame your tigers. As a consultant, I have been able to gather essential information by actively listening and acting on what I perceive. Consultants are rarely called into businesses that are functioning at 100% perfection, right? So you can imagine the angry managers, employees, and customers I might encounter at any given business; I have encountered plenty of tigers who were ready to pounce!

In fact, one business location where I was contracted had a *very* irate customer. She had tried unsuccessfully to address her concerns with management, so she took it upon herself to round up a streak of customers to descend on the office when they heard there was a new consultant in town.

The ringmaster for this event was also the self-appointed spokesperson, and most of the group was silent with the exception of this fine tiger. I am glad to report that all ended well with no shots fired. I later learned that the entire scene had been staged by a disgruntled employee who was the subject of a disciplinary action my client requested I complete for them. Oh, those disgruntled tigers!

Listen to your tigers!

I had been listening for tigers as I always do from the moment I walked into the business. But this one was so cunning and connected that she pulled off the affair in a matter of a few hours. Due to the mistrust shown by the disgruntled employee, my client decided to make the disgruntled employee a newly terminated employee (and I agreed). Sadly, her biggest tiger was the one she saw in the mirror every morning.

The moral of the story? Unfortunately, all 'tigers' can't be anticipated or saved. When they attack the organization with the sole intent of doing harm, it says something about their soul, about their inner being and about their core values. They are a danger that can't be trusted. Always be listening and be aware of the unseen dangers that have the potential to pounce upon you without notice.

Ask, Listen and Apply. Repeat as Necessary.
In most cases, however, by listening to people's issues and concerns with focus and awareness, I may be able to learn in short order what action needs to be taken to fix that business. I am no genius, but I have trained myself to perceive clearly what people say and, sometimes even more important, what they *don't* say. Usually, people

will tell you very clearly what they need if you ask them. Then it's up to you to carefully consider their motives and answers.

At the risk of putting myself and my consulting peers out of business, let me share with you that *you* can do this, too! *Ask* questions, *listen* to the answers, and then *apply* what you learn as you *implement* actions based on what your tigers have taught you. Be aware, however, if you try this on your own turf. Oftentimes you will gain more information by having an independent third party do the analysis. So I guess those consultants still have a place in our corporate jungle, don't they?

Stumbling Blocks to Perception & Awareness
Few people hone their skills in perception and awareness because few of them listen well. Some try, but they are easily distracted or don't focus - they simply don't know *how* to listen – while others tune out or don't bother, as they are convinced that they know better or they see no point in it.

Also, many if not most of us have seen a lot of negative reinforcement. That exposure can cause us to become entrenched in our own opinions. We commit to our own ideas and are determined that our way is the right way, the only way. If we're not open to others' opinions, it's safe to say that we're not going to listen very attentively to them.

Yes, some people are very good at *pretending* to listen and will even sit patiently for lengthy periods of time 'listening', but when it is their turn to talk they couch the discussion in their own terms, not in what they have just heard.

Finally, many people suffer from the mistaken notion that to gain and maintain power and authority, they must always know what to do, and if they don't know, they fake it, so as to never appear weak. To those people, asking questions, listening, and communicating are signs of weakness.

But those individuals are wrong. When you exclude others' opinions, you ignore important, valuable information. When you exclude knowledge, you exclude the potential for the greatest results.

When you ask questions and actively listen to the answers with the intention of making changes to benefit everyone, you respect those you listen to; they will perceive that respect and will, in turn, respect you. And there's no weakness in respect, is there?

Your tigers take a risk when they go out on a limb and speak the truth to you. They can only unmask if they perceive that you are trustworthy, respectful, and able to achieve results.

Dan Stockdale

NOTES

Taming Tigers

Dan Stockdale

Chapter 13: Taming Tigers Secret #5 (continued)

Perception & Awareness - Part 2: Success Follows Focus

In the wild, a tiger's goals are pretty simple and straightforward – to eat, sleep, and procreate. Rough life, huh? Well, actually it is! Let's talk about eating for a minute. We all perceive tigers as majestic, powerful, dominating creatures. But they fail to achieve their goal – to get the kill – an incredible 95% of the time. With those odds, eating can be quite a challenge!

> Tigers actually <u>fail</u> to capture and kill their prey more than 90% of the time!

If eating is that much trouble, surely sleeping is a breeze, right? Well, not exactly. Mature male tigers are always at risk of displacement by a younger male who wants to take over his territory. Hours spent sleeping can result in losing his kingdom.

Okay, if eating is a challenge and sleeping can change a tiger's position in life, surely procreation is simple! When it comes to the wild, don't assume anything. A tiger can breed successfully and have cute cubs frolicking about in the tall grass of the savannah. But, remember that young male tiger I just mentioned? Well, if he successfully displaces the male, he will likely kill the frolicking cubs so that he can start his *own* genetic line.

For a tiger, achieving the goals of eating, sleeping, and procreating requires tremendous focus. For us two-legged creatures to focus on a goal, we must first determine the outcome we want from *our* tigers. When I train an animal, I have a certain goal in mind and a training plan to reach that goal. I don't take a tiger out and ask him, "What are we going to do today?" and then sort of improvise from there.

Trainers know that the tiger has a particular scene in a movie or a photo shoot coming up, so they need to train the tiger to lunge safely at a person, for example. The training plan will elaborate on all of the steps needed in order to safely achieve the behavior. It provides a goal to focus on and the steps to achieve that goal.

Be Wildly Successful in Your Environment
Always look for ways to use your environment to help you achieve your goals. Tigers in the wild use bushes, trees, and tall grass to help them reach their target. As a matter of fact, unlike your lap cat that cringes at the sight of water, tigers actually enjoy playing in water and will use it as a place to hide while stalking their prey. We call that behavior "crocodile" because they will completely submerge themselves except for their eyes and the top of their head – very reminiscent of the image of crocodiles you frequently see on TV.

What about *your* environment? What is in *your* environment that you can use to help maintain your focus and achieve your goals? Hopefully you are not trying to ambush employees who are easy prey. But are there certain things about your work environment that you can utilize to be more successful or maintain better focus? If you, like I, have difficulty focusing with constant interruptions and noise, could you change your environment by simply shutting the door to your office for a certain period of time each day? Yes, I know about and agree with an "open door policy", but you have to be able to work without interruption sometime!

If your goal is to increase performance in the accounting department, can you rearrange the office so that everyone's computer screens are easily seen by others? Could that additional bit of accountability possibly increase productivity?

Just as tigers will use their environment to most benefit them, there are many ways to use your environment to enhance your benefit as well.

What is Your Perception of Success?
When trainers embark on training an animal to perform a behavior - whether it's simply getting the critter into a carrier to be taken to the

vet, or training a bald eagle to fly from the top of the Super Bowl stadium to land on the goal line as "The Star Spangled Banner" ends with a crescendo - there is a goal.

Success and goals are inextricably linked. To successfully attain goals, everyone involved must be focused on them. Obviously, to move forward, you must know what you're aiming for, even if it's just a deadline.

Successfully achieving your goals involves perception and awareness in several ways. You've probably heard the saying "Success isn't a destination; it's a journey"? It's true! Many individuals and families have achieved considerable financial success. If "success" were a destination, these individuals would take their money, retire on the beach, and live happily ever after. But that's not the case. They continue to work, they continue to have vision, and they continue to have goals. Apparently they enjoy the journey!

The success they attain along the way, however, has most likely come as a matter of their keen perception and awareness as they fought, day-by-day, to reach their initial goals as they venture down the pathway of their jungle.

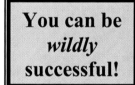

You see, oftentimes we may begin our journey toward success down one path, then find that another path may actually lead to greater achievements. Then as we go along this trail for a while, we may find yet another even more lucrative and attractive path.

If you don't perceive possibilities to change your course as you progress, you may find that you will not achieve the success you could have had if you had been more aware of all of the other opportunities that surround you. You may miss a potentially huge success because you failed to be attentive and observant.

Life truly is an adventure! The expedition matters and *how* and *what* you learn on the journey determines your success. To be certain, you *must* have goals to focus on so you know exactly where you're headed. If you do, you will get there, and then the *next* goal appears, and you focus on it.

But remain perceptive and aware; true success is not a place in life where you ultimately arrive. Success is a journey down a path with many twists, turns and diversions. The trip has many hidden trails, crossroads, and difficult to see paths. Be aware of what lies ahead and perceptive enough to see beyond the next curve. And be willing to roll with the diversions. In the end, you'll find that those who are truly successful are the adventurers who have taken moments to create a positive impact on those lives they have touched along the journey.

Be perceptive. Be aware. Be willing. Be a difference maker.

NOTES

Dan Stockdale

Chapter 13: Taming Tigers Secret #5 (continued)

Perception & Awareness - Part 3: Dress for Tiger Taming Success

Others' perception *of you* is just as important as your own perceptions. Can you imagine sitting at the circus, the show is about to conclude with the finale – a tiger act with half a dozen tigers. The music is building and the ringmaster steps up into the center of a cascade of four spotlights that are now shining on the middle of the arena, "Ladies and Gentleman! Boys and Girls of all ages. The greatest spectacle known to mankind. They are fierce with the ability to kill! They roam the earth looking for prey! And they are here today to perform for you in one special show! Now, please welcome the man who has no fear and who works with these beasts! Please welcome the fearless tiger tamer himself, *(insert your favorite animal trainer's name here)*!

As all four spotlights sweep to the far end of the arena amid a spectacular chorus of harmonious trumpets, we see the star of the show walking through the curtains! No, I don't mean he walks through a split in the curtains. I mean he walks *through* the curtains. He couldn't find the opening he was supposed to walk through so he pushes on the curtain until the bottom of it brushes over his head as he stoops down to enter the arena.

As the spotlights settle on him, the world-renowned tiger trainer nonchalantly walks toward the enclosure that hold the tigers. His hair looks as if he just got out of bed. You notice him wearing a tattered t-shirt from some remote city and tattered shorts with well-worn, untied tennis shoes. As he continues his casual stroll toward the tiger enclosure, he yawns and stretches.

No, it is not part of the act. He just rolled out of bed a few minutes ago and ambled into the arena from his trailer 50 feet outside the backstage entrance. He's obviously tired but, what the heck, he might as well give this a whirl. As he walks, he is thinking, "What city is this anyhow?" and, "I wonder what's for supper in catering?"

Amidst the introduction, trumpets, and fanfare we were expecting a well-groomed, practiced, polished, professional fully clad in a sequined costume and sporting all of the self-confidence of a man who knows how to work with 500 pound killers! This guy can't help but disappoint, can he?

So, what does your "costume" look like? Do you *look* like a confident, competent tiger tamer? You are, after all, constantly being judged by others, especially initially, based upon your appearance, not your performance or capabilities. Before our sleepy-headed circus trainer came near his tigers, the audience already had a quickly conceived conclusion about him and his ability, didn't they?

Do we generally see the President of the United States on TV in jeans and a t-shirt, or does he look the personification of The President? He could be the greatest political mind of the century, yet people would find it very difficult to take him seriously if he was standing behind a podium in the Rose Garden in shorts.

> Real tigers dress for success! A tiger's skin has the same stripe pattern as their coat.

When you go to the garage to get your car serviced, does the mechanic roll out from under the car wearing a suit? When was the last time you saw a landscaper digging around in a flower bed in her evening gown?

My point is simply this: your confidence, conduct, and appearance must be appropriate for *at least* the position you hold, and preferably one level up. So, if you are a cook, and your goal is to be a sous chef, start dressing a notch above what the other cooks are wearing. Be sure your uniform is crisp, clean, and even starched. Be polished and package yourself so that your supervisors begin to perceive you in a different light, a cut above your peers, as a chef, not a cook.

This is one area where we humans have a distinct advantage over tigers. You've heard the expressions, "A leopard can't change its spots," right? Well, it's the same for tigers. Try as they may, tigers have a tough time putting on a new coat. As a matter of fact, if you were to shave off all of a tiger's hair (if you ever try, I want to watch – from outside the enclosure!), there would still be stripes on its skin because it bears the pigment in a pattern that matches each tiger's individual stripes. Deep inside, they may aspire to be a grizzly bear, but they will never look like one. A tiger's uniform can't be changed.

So, what does your costume say about you, your aspirations, your position, or your desire to advance? Do you look like a tiger tamer?

Our own perceptions and awareness of ourselves are essential to our ability to successfully tame our tigers. Similarly, the way *others* perceive us helps to determine whether they will join us in our quest to meet our goals.

Now let's look at a tiger taming principle that pervades all of them: *balance* and *control*.

Dan Stockdale

TIGER TALKING POINTS

1. What is a defining moment?

2. What have been the defining moments in your life?

3. Does the positive model always work?

Taming Tigers

Dan Stockdale

Dan monkeying around with a macaque!

Chapter 14: Taming Tigers Secret #6

Balance & Control

> *"My dreams come from God and God has*
> *the power to accomplish them!"*
> *-Julia Cameron*

Believe it or not, it's fairly easy to remain calm when training real tigers, because trainers rapidly learn that, in a training or performance situation, negative behavior from an animal is rarely a personal attack on their connection with the animal. Most tiger trainers who are injured will tell you that the animal likely did *not* intend to hurt them as a result of some aberrant aspect of their relationship; an injured trainer will probably tell you that he or she made a mistake.

Safety-conscious tiger trainers maintain balance and control in their relationships with their animals at all times. Real tigers are one thing, but remaining calm, holding your temper, or thinking rationally can be much more difficult with human tigers. Our human tigers have a way of getting under our skin, right? It seems like those closest to us, at home and at work, have the greatest ability to enrage *our* inner tiger.

Dan Stockdale

As you read about balance and control, think of *your* tigers and the ways you can maintain balance and control in your relationship with them. Consider how things will be different once you achieve true balance in the relationship.

Adaptability & Flexibility: Picking Your Battles
Flexibility in the training environment means being flexible in your approach to meeting the needs of the particular animal. If certain cues or rewards aren't working with an animal, the trainer will try others. One tiger may learn well in an area that is in close proximity to other tigers and is not ever distracted by them; another tiger may have to have a quiet, more isolated area for training sessions. It is obviously inflexible (and therefore ineffective) to say, "Well, this is the training area we *always* use to train Point A to Point B behavior, so this is the one *all* animals must use."

How does the principle of flexibility apply to *your* tigers? A common tiger you may encounter are very regimented and structured people who see issues strictly in black and white, without shades of gray. Instead of trying to direct your tiger towards a certain behavior, you could say, "Well, what do you think of X?" Or "How can we adapt and work the situation to achieve the ultimate goal, but with standards that are a little less rigid for right now, so we can move the entire organization in the right direction? Then, gradually implement the more stringent standards we all want to ultimately see?"

As with flexibility, having this adaptability offers a strength far greater than mindlessly following along with the corporate cookie-cutter mentality that exists largely because of fear of cutting against the grain of corporate culture or out of fear of litigation. But consider this: in a courtroom, if you have to explain why you made a change and adapted a certain policy for an individual, most juries and judges are rational individuals who will accept a decision made in good faith. Sure, we can all point to decisions of aberrant juries, but it is not the norm.

I have been in management for more than 2 decades, practicing this sort of adaptability for most of that time, and I have only had one employee lawsuit. The original suit was for a quarter of a million dollars. It settled out of court for a nominal amount because the cost of defense was higher than the settlement cost.

But nearly everybody in business has a healthy dose of corporate culture or legal paranoia, and obviously you must be careful. Consider what's going on in your organization and industry, and the circumstances that have bearing on the situation. But by and large in terms of day-to-day operations, you should be able to adapt when and if appropriate. If one employee complains about favoritism being shown to another – which is typically how the principle of adaptability will be challenged – you can stand behind your decisions and know that you have consistently applied a fair standard of adaptability across the board for all employees of all ages, sex, religions and races.

When the Media Calls, Avoid Being Your Own Worst Tiger

Few qualities are as compelling to others – in a tiger trainer or anyone else – as calm confidence. But sometimes, we can be our own worst tiger by letting situations affect us emotionally, not maintaining a calm, matter-of-fact approach, at least where we need to the most, with an audience of peers, employees, or the community at large. By remaining calm and in control, you help others to do so, and you can prevent even the most heated emotional situation from reaching an even more critical point.

In your leadership role, those within your tribe will react largely based upon the communication they receive from you, both verbal and written. But even greater is the effect of your non-verbals: your posture, your confidence, your internal fortitude. If you are calm, confident and poised, you will breathe calmness, confidence and poise into those around you. They will draw assurance from your leadership – from the traits you communicate both verbally and non-verbally.

Dan Stockdale

Likewise, if your organization is facing adversity and you as a leader are unsettled, I can assure you that those around you will be ill at ease as well.

Consider the images of executives on the news: one who appears very calm and self-confident, another who appears very nervous, as if his or her confidence is shaken. What differences do these two people communicate to the viewing audience? How is that transferred to the workplace, in terms of employees' perception of the boss?

What type of image do *you* send out to your audience, when circumstances become stressful?

- o Are you able to deal with difficult situations in a calm manner?
- o Can you divorce your personal feelings from the situation and maintain a professional perspective?
- o How do you keep your cool when you feel personally threatened or when you are about to exhibit an uncontrollable emotional response?
- o Are you able to bring your rationality to the fore?

Or could you afford to learn a few tips from real tiger tamers that may help you look cool and controlled in stressful situations? Most of us could, frankly, and lucky for you, 3Ts has those tips at your disposal!

Staying Calm, Cool, and Collected
My personal method for remaining calm under pressure, and I have seen it work wonders for others, too, is to maintain focus on the issue, not on the people or emotions involved, in as personable a manner as possible.

Here are some other ideas:

- o *If you need to walk away, walk away.* Find a reason to get out of the situation for a moment to quickly think through the situation. This can make a world of difference in your ability to collect your thoughts and form a plan, and will save you from a public meltdown in the bargain. If a tiger trainer needs to leave the arena for a few moments, that's fine! Better to leave and return composed than for your tigers to sense your apprehension.

o *When the heat is on or there is a possibility of impending legal issues, restrict as much contact as possible to a written form of communication.* If your position means you will have to deal with the media, written responses allow an answer that is worded exactly the way you want it to be and offers the added benefit of a paper trail.

o *Deal with the media on your schedule.* If a reporter calls wanting a quote right away, simply say, "I am in the middle of a meeting right now. Let me get back to you within half an hour or so, and then I will be glad to talk." Then take that time to think through your response and jot down notes. This will allow you to present a calm and controlled public perception and will prevent you from saying things that end up in print that you wish you'd said more thoughtfully and with planning.

Maintain a calm approach, no matter how out of control the situation. Rarely will the public need to know the minute details of the day-to-day struggles you may be facing; that is a separate matter to which you can apply your calm demeanor after initial damage control.

Remain Calm at all Costs
Even in situations where tensions are running high, but that aren't a train wreck waiting to happen – such as a meeting where participants have personal agendas working at cross-

Real tiger trainers know how to adjust quickly to get the result they want. You should too!

purposes – there, also, calm is key. You can't get caught up in even minor chaos or the situation may devolve into *major* chaos. You, or whoever is conducting the meeting, has to maintain a level head. If the leader starts going down the emotional hatch with the rest of the group, then the whole system completely falls apart.

Just as real tiger trainers know how to adjust quickly to get the result they want, an effective leader is able to maintain calm and gently redirect the meeting back on track.

Machete Management - Foraging a Path Through Dense Foliage
Let's take a look at using 3Ts in worse case scenarios to remain calm in a true crisis.

If your jungle is overgrown with foliage and grave, impending dangers lurk in the shadows, you may need to implement *machete management*, using a figurative machete to clear the pathway of dense underbrush to reach a meadow where you can see the light of day.

If a business is in crisis mode - under intense regulatory or media scrutiny, experiencing extreme financial pressure, or infested with employees who aren't producing - then management must act quickly. Leaders may even have to leap into a punishment and negative reinforcement mode to initiate abrupt change so they may avert a crisis or even extinction of the entire organization. Machete management isn't fun but is sometimes the only thing that will give a glimmer of hope for organizational survival.

- If you are an executive in a health care organization, and state and federal regulators in your facility are threatening to close the doors or evacuate the building, it just may be time for machete management.

- If you are in the C-suite of a Fortune 1000 company, and you find out the CFO has been cooking the books, it may be time for machete management.

- If you're walking to your car at the end of the day, and are greeted by a reporter with a microphone asking you about a death caused minutes earlier by your newly released, much-touted toddler toy, it may be time for machete management.

If you are the health care executive in the example above, what machete management measures might you implement? It may involve insisting that your executive team take rotating shifts 24/7 to ensure patient care improves rapidly. You could lock your executive staff out of their offices and insist they visit every patient every day to assess current conditions. The executive team could also meet with medical and nursing teams daily or even hourly to assess vulnerabilities, needs, and progress.

If our book-cooking CFO has been successful in draining the company's reservoir of financial resources, machete management may involve pay cuts, benefit cuts, layoffs, or other drastic measures.

When you are in the midst of a business crisis, the business as a whole may seem too far gone to adopt a positive model. But tread lightly: it may just be that *some* operating practices are ineffective or *some* employees are too far gone to respond to positive reinforcement practices. If that's the case, you simply need to make a few tough decisions rather than sacrificing the entire business. However, as the operation is getting back on track, it is vital to revert your management style back to the positive approach of 3Ts.

Calm and Control: A Killer Combination
By control here, I mean maintaining control over the environment and the particular situation in which you find yourself. When a trainer is working with a tiger outside its enclosure, you now know that they work with at least one partner. If there are other people around, we have to control how close they come to the animal, who goes into which areas and when, when the tiger's coming out of the enclosure to go to a work area, and the people who may be watching.

Dan Stockdale

Tiger trainers work in teams, and the tiger is a major component of that team. Even the team concept offers an element of control. For safety's sake, one person works on a behavior and the other holds the cat and takes it back to the start position to begin a new behavior. The trainer constantly controls every minute detail as to who has the door, who has the cat, what direction the other trainer is going with the cat, when the door is closing, if there is a sudden change of plans, what is happening outside the arena, how might the cat react, what would be your response if the tiger reacted in that manner, and so forth.

In order to maintain control, a trainer must be actively thinking through all possibilities, regardless of how unlikely, at all times.

Balancing Control Without Tipping Over Into Rigidity
You may wonder how this level of minute control can work in the business environment, though, without becoming rigid, which we know we don't want, right? Well, that's where balance comes in.

Balance occurs when you have parameters everybody operates within, but are flexible within those parameters. It may be easier to think of it as "direction," rather than control, for purposes of this discussion. Obviously, everyone - and perhaps most especially managers - want to feel like they are in control, but being in *calm control* and being a *control freak* are two different things.

As you've learned, one of the most important aspects of 3Ts is *balance*. You can use positive reinforcement through 3Ts and still be in charge. Just because you have exercised flexibility with an employee over a deadline that you had the power to adjust, does not make you a weak manager. Actually, it shows your strength and power because you had the ability to make the change and you did in order to ultimately get the results you wanted.

You are in control and you presumably used your authority for the right reasons. You used your influence to create a situation where you and the organization win *and* the employee wins. Balance and control go inseparably hand-in-hand.

Work Smart, Not Hard

Your environment must be balanced as well. All work and no play makes you a dull boy or girl. Your ability to achieve balance in your environment is just as important at home as it is at work. If you are working 60 hours a week, you are *sacrificing* something in another area of your life to do so. Maybe you're sacrificing your love for hiking, time with your spouse or child, or a desire to volunteer at the local animal shelter.

You may think you're doing your organization a favor by sacrificing your time at the altar of the business, but in most cases quite the contrary is true. Study after study shows that those who work exhausting hours are actually less productive than their counterparts who have the ability to balance *all* of the varying priorities in their lives.

A report in *Circadian* at http://www.circadian.com/media/ 2003_press_overtime.htm cites "studies showing that productivity in manufacturing operations, as measured by output per hour, declines as overtime increases. This is particularly true when overtime is distributed unevenly. One study cited states that a 10% increase in overtime on average results in a 2.4% *decrease* in productivity."

"More output is achieved, but the number of hours worked per employee also increases, resulting in a lower output per hour," explained Kerin, author of the *Circadian* report.

Furthermore, in white collar jobs, some studies have shown that performance can decrease by as much a 25% when workers put in 60 or more hours per week for prolonged periods of time.

Kerin attributed the loss in productivity to greater mental and physical fatigue among workers. As more time is allocated to complete a task, the work rate tends to slow and unproductive time increases, he noted. Concerns over work/family balance and health problems may lead to a phenomenon experts refer to as "presenteeism," where an employee is physically at work, but his mind is not on the job.

Dan Stockdale

A recent article by the International Game Developers Association at http://www.igda.org/articles/erobinson_crunch.php states "most industries gave up crunch mode over 75 years ago: It is the single most expensive way there is to get the work done." It goes on to state that "More than a century of studies show that long-term useful worker output is maximized near a five-day, 40-hour workweek. Productivity drops immediately upon starting overtime and continues to drop until, at approximately eight 60-hour weeks, the total work done is the same as what would have been done in eight 40-hour weeks."

Avoid Imbalance, but not with More Work!
If your life is out of balance, and you are working excessively, you may be running from something that you don't want to face. You may think you are toiling away *for* the business when in fact are practicing *avoidance behavior*. Regardless of why you are doing it, excessive work inevitably leads to imbalance.

Think of it in these terms: If we were trying to train an animal to perform a behavior, maybe sitting up and swatting with her foot, do you think we would do well teaching the behavior if we worked with her for 10-15 minutes? What about if we dragged the training session out to an hour or two? Do you think that we would get to a point where both trainer and tiger were getting frustrated? Or, how about if we continued the training session for 8 or 10 hours? How would our 'productivity' be? Do you think we would have a ticked off tiger on our hands? You bet!

Whether you are the CEO of a Fortune 100 company, a retiree volunteer, or a tiger trainer teaching an animal a behavior for a movie for the very first time, seek balance in your life.

Roll With It!
I had an acquaintance who was in her early 80s and she was talking about a gentleman she knows who had just celebrated his 100th birthday. She asked him, "What's your secret?" and he said, "I go

with the flow." That is a simple philosophy for all of us to follow. Just roll with it!

Too, when training tigers, you can't hyper-focus on minor issues, making a big deal out of small situations. For example, one facility I trained at has a separate housing area for its animals where they sleep and spend their leisure time. If I were planning to take a tiger to the working arena, we would walk down a path that would take us in front of another work area.

If the tiger I was walking suddenly noticed that another trainer had a couple of animals in the arena working them, we would let her stop and take a look. We'd roll with it and never force her to move along.

Part of 'rolling with it' is choosing your battles. If she wants to stop and hang out for a minute or two and watch the other animals as they do behaviors, that is okay. And after she loses interest in that, then we move on down toward our work area.

> Roll with it! It can add years to your life and can yield exceptional results.

Now, you may be the hard-charging corporate type who equates "rolling with it" to getting flushed down the toilet of business! I'm certainly not saying to disregard structure, policy, and standard operating procedures. I am suggesting, however, that true leaders see the big picture and have the savvy to adjust and compromise as needed to achieve the overall organizational goals. Yes, leaders are concerned about the details, but they don't *live in* the details. They adjust as necessary.

If the chairman of the board isn't willing to be somewhat flexible, to go with the flow to a degree, the board would be a dictatorship and there wouldn't be much use for the other members, would there?

Yes, we all have experienced boards that were manipulated as dictatorships, where the board was expected to rubber stamp the singular interests of a particular individual. And sometimes that individual is so slick that he or she actually convinces the board members that they have been a participant in the decision-making process.

But at the end of the day, the boards that operate with an autocrat's approach, that only have a singular focus, that don't 'roll with it' to explore all options - these boards and organizations suffer. Maybe the autocrat in charge feels successful and fulfilled, but to these types, it is about power, not the good of the organization.

Pick Your Battles in All Aspects of Life
In your own life and work, you may know that you shouldn't become overly concerned over the minor annoyances that crop up, or overemphasize what doesn't really matter. But that can be easier said than done, and you may feel unable to help yourself from making mountains out of molehills.

I have often seen managers obsess over a minor issue that, in the grand scheme, is totally irrelevant; then their behavior easily ends up driving off a very valuable employee. Because of this minor issue, and the manager's fixation on it, the organization suffers and the employee suffers. So I will say it again: be willing to go with the flow whenever you can and pick your battles with intellectual thoughtfulness, not emotion.

When you find yourself becoming stressed over a situation, ask yourself, "Is it really going to matter a year from now, or five years from now?" If it's not, then in THE BIG PICTURE, it's not a huge deal. Don't give it more weight than it deserves.

Remember in Principle #4 - Motivation when we discussed Karen, the salesperson who couldn't meet her quota for the month? I suggested ways her sales manager might help her that differed from the usual negative sales management strategies of threats and abuse.

The principles of balance and control offer the same ideas for that situation: Instead of the ultimately futile behavior of *pushing* somebody to get out of a sales slump, acknowledge the reality of the slump and *move on*, looking at next month, where there is an opportunity to get a jumpstart on the quota.

A tiger trainer doesn't get overly concerned over a missed cue or failure to achieve a behavior perfectly every time. Instead, the trainer rolls with it focusing on consistently applying 3Ts to achieve results and, ultimately, success!

Practice Patience

Animals learn at different paces, and you can't push to try to control the learning process; trainers know this and allow them the time to be in their own rhythm with the learning. If a trainer were to push a tiger during training, he or she would skew the learning curve so that it would actually take longer for the tiger to learn the behavior. If a trainer were to push an animal, the environment would be uncomfortable and not relaxed, so the animal would grow anxious and naturally can't learn as quickly. Forcing the process is counterproductive and self-defeating. Thus, the trainer knows to be patient, and to let the process go at its natural pace.

In the workplace, managers certainly have tasks they want and need to accomplish; sometimes, it helps to step back, take a breather, and allow the process time to work versus constantly forcing the push toward your goal, trying to control that which is beyond control. You may want instant results, and get frustrated when a deadline has not been met, for example. But you have to recognize that there is a learning curve and be as patient as circumstances permit.

What if you are frustrated, feeling that your staff should have learned by now the information or skill you have been training them in? How do you know when you need to try another approach, even negative reinforcement, versus when to keep patiently plugging away?

Let's look at an example of just such a dilemma – and let me warn you, I am going to tell you that you need *balance*!

Imagine that you're an airplane manufacturer, and you sign an order for a client who wants to buy a jet. You're working that process through engineering and then operations, manufacturing and production to actually get the aircraft built. If you try to rush that process to the point that you are compromising the safety of the aircraft, you are going too far. Yet, by the same token, you have promised a delivery date to this customer; you must balance - being patient with the engineering and production process so you don't get a result you don't want – a crashed airplane – with the client's needs for an on-time delivery.

Balance is easier, even patience itself is easier to exercise, if you have spent time getting prepared and organized. You're going to be more prone to be patient if you have accurately estimated the time it would take to manufacture the plane…though less prone to patience if you underestimated the time in order to get the sale. You will still have to be patient with those unexpected circumstances – and plan time in the schedule for unexpected delays from the beginning - but generally, you will have a good sense of what to expect and can go with the flow better.

Learning When to Cut Your Losses
In some situations, neither positive reinforcement, negative reinforcement, nor punishment is going to make a difference.

Circumstances can arise where no one is at fault, but ties must be cut nonetheless, difficult as that may be. I have had employees working for me from time to time who were good people, but, for whatever reason, they were in the wrong position at the wrong time; working in my organization was not a good fit for them. As difficult as it can be from a humanitarian perspective, sometimes you have to cut your losses so that the organization can progress.

Sometimes, an animal is simply unable to function in a certain environment, and its trainer must find an alternative. For example, a few years ago I was training an owl monkey named Mango for a role in my speaking events. A few months into the relationship, I developed a severe allergy to him, probably in reaction to his dander or his urine. After trying several medications and other treatments, it became apparent that I could no longer have contact with him. He returned home to Florida and is living a very happy life with several other owl monkeys. Although it was a heart-wrenching experience, it was best for us both.

The need to cut your losses may develop for many reasons. I have often seen people in positions for which they were technically qualified and competent but the interpersonal relationships they should have developed so the team could gel simply didn't happen. As a result, petty differences and bickering eventually interfered with business.

Dan Stockdale

TIGER TALKING POINTS

1. Why should you listen to squeaky wheels?

2. When is it okay to cut your losses with an employee?

Lions, tigers and bears!

Chapter 15: Taming Tigers Secret #7

Conservation

"It's a funny thing about life; if you refuse to accept anything but the best, you very often get it."
-Somerset Maugham

There are more tigers in captivity in the United States than exist in the wild in the rest of the world.

Wild tigers need a relationship with mankind too, albeit in a different way. The poignant part about the "wild" is that the majority of the tigers we classify as living 'in the wild' are actually living in tiger *preserves* where poachers, local farmers, and villagers frequently trespass to kill the tigers. As a matter of fact, on average, one tiger per day is killed in the wild.

And local farmers frequently encroach upon the tiger preserves themselves, clearing the trees and grazing their cattle. Unless there is a drastic change, the demise of the tiger in any natural environments appears eminent.

Dan Stockdale

Just as we need to steadfastly guard our relationships with tigers in the wild, tigers in captivity need a different type of relationship with humans. They also need our compassion and understanding, whether they live half a world away in the "wild," or half a mile away at the local zoo. Of course, directors of preserves and trainers who are responsible for tigers in captivity must possess an extra sense of calling to the profession to keep up with the demands and to constantly put the animals' needs ahead of their own.

Those who are responsible for tigers' well-being must work relentlessly on building their relationship with the tigers within their care; whether the relationship is the personal relationship of a trainer or the official relationship of a preserve director.

As you have read the preceding pages of this book, I hope that you come away with a newfound appreciation for conservation: of your personal life, of your business, and of the tiger. Regardless of how established and imposing an animal or corporation is, it can face extinction at a moment's notice. If your eyes aren't peeled toward conserving your organization, it is *endangered*!

You've seen vast organizations that have survived for decades on the verge of collapse. It doesn't matter how big your organization is or how long you've been in business. You can even be a household name. But if you're not focused on conservation of your organization, you are in jeopardy of becoming extinct.

If our eyes as a society aren't attentive to the precarious status of some species in our environment that are at risk, they will become extinct. We have a duty to protect.

You see, our world community is ever-expanding, and as our world population increases, we extend our communities and incessantly infringe on the territory of our animal cohabitants.

It is a delicate balancing act: growth and conservation. Sometimes they are in direct competition with each other. Other times we find a way to make them coexist in relative harmony.

Conservation is a common need in our businesses and our environment. Develop a conservation plan for your business so that you never run the risk of extinction.

Dan Stockdale

NOTES

Dan speaking right before the animals come out!

Chapter 16: Conclusion

Will You Flinch?

"Surround yourself with people who respect and treat you well."
-Claudia Black

Walking Toby – Will You Flinch?
On a movie set where Toby was living, I was preparing to take him for a walk at the end of our shoot. I was a new face to Toby, and he was a new face to me. This was our first day together. The gravel path at the top of the hill was wide and stretched out before us for several hundred feet, curving past numerous, very large tiger enclosures that were spread across a grassy hillside – with an abundance of room for tigers to play.

As we began our journey down the trail, Toby momentarily turned his head directly toward me, looking me straight in the eye, then snarled, showing his massive teeth. He was testing me. He wanted to see what I was made of. He was asking me, "Will you flinch? Can I make you uncomfortable? Can I be in charge here?" I didn't respond. I didn't break my stride. No, Toby, I will not flinch.

As you play the role you have been given in life, you too will be tested. You will have employees who don't agree with you, regardless of your leadership style. You will have supervisors who want you to perform more, even if you're the number one salesperson in the company. You will have customers who attempt to shake your ethical staying power. In short, you will have *tigers* that attempt to make you flinch – that want to see what you are made of. They will even try their best to intimidate you. When that happens, will you flinch?

In order to tame, or train, the largest killer cats on the planet, you now know that it's not accomplished by brute strength and nerves of steel. Coming on too strong will get you killed. You have learned that the secret is in *relationships* and how you manage those relationships both individually and collectively. Work on your relationships. Build them to greatness! Create alliances with those who support you, those who will work with you and who share your vision, and yes, even those who challenge you.

Work hard to achieve balance in all areas of your life. Remember, not only does "too much work make Jack a dull boy", it also lowers your on-the-job performance as well as your productivity. Your family and friends deserve to have their share of you too. When the role you're in now is but a distant memory you will find that your friends and family are what matters. Achieve balance.

Remember, too, that you have the ability to change your role. If you're not happy with the circumstances you are in, you can fire your employer, even if you're the CEO. You can make the changes necessary to make your role in this world one that is meaningful to you and one that has a tremendous impact on your universe. The only thing that stands between you and the leadership success you have always dreamed of is *your* desire to have an impact.

A couple final notes regarding success. Remember, success isn't a location or a single point in time. Success is the *manner* in which you make your expedition through this life. Don't naively believe that someone is going to come up to you at some point in your career and christen you as a "success." True success, or failure, happens day-by-day in how you conduct yourself in your dealings with others. Success lies in the knowledge that you are filling the role on this earth that you were intended to fulfill. It is in acting with honesty and integrity in every encounter you have with those in your tribe. It is in the *relationships* you successfully create and sustain. Does this describe you? If so, you are indeed a success!

Finally, don't fall into the trap of measuring your success by the amount of money in your bank account, the number of toys you acquire, or the amount of power you can garner. In the end, frankly, none of these things matter.

I have seen millions made, and I have seen millions lost. I have had access to corporate planes and even owned a few of my own. I have owned fine cars, fine houses, fine clothes, and I have seen some of the most spectacular places in our country. And, at the end of the day, none of it is of any value to me. I only achieved success in my life when I was able to wed my two passions: exotic animals and business.

I have a unique life. Nowadays, I let the suits hang in my closet in silence as I spend most days in khakis with my sleeves rolled up. Many days are spent cleaning out enclosures and getting an occasional challenge from some exotic critter as well as creating ways to share my lessons from exotic animals to the world of business. Yes, I have been bitten and scratched by various beasts, but nothing serious. I spend a lot of time on planes visiting different facilities, learning from other trainers, and attending conventions. I will always be a trainer in training, always seeking to learn more. You should be too.

To be sure, I love corporate America, and I enjoy every opportunity I get, every invitation I receive, to venture back into that world to consult or speak. Hopefully, I now have an even greater impact on more people than I ever have in the past when I worked with small groups of people for extended periods of time.

And I am doing my best to continually develop a presentation that will teach organizations how to improve their leadership skills, sales success and corporate culture by applying a few techniques that are used every day by exotic animal trainers around the globe. With any luck, those I encounter not only learn how to better *manage* their organizations, they also acquire a newfound *appreciation* for their organization as well as for conservation of our earth's endangered species.

I get to work with exotic animals, and I get to help organizations become better places and make more money. What more could I ask for in a career? I am a very blessed man, and I have never been happier in my life!

Of course, like you, around every bend, I am always finding new "tigers" to tame. Sometimes they are real tigers - sometimes they are the corporate kind - and sometimes I realize that the tiger I need to tame most that day is me.

Let me challenge you to tame your tigers, too, and to achieve your own personal success. Always remember the Tiger Taming Techniques you have learned and apply them kindly within your world whenever possible. Don't sell yourself short and never be afraid to attain the success you were predestined to achieve! I believe in you, and I know you will succeed in achieving your goals!

Now, go tame *your* tigers!

Dan Stockdale